PROPHETS & PROPHECY

PROPHETS & PROPHECY

JOSEPH FIELDING McCONKIE

BOOKCRAFT
Salt Lake City, Utah

Copyright © 1988 by Bookcraft, Inc.

All rights reserved. This book or any part thereof may not be reproduced in any form whatsoever, whether by graphic, visual, electronic, filming, microfilming, tape recording, or any other means, without the prior written permission of Bookcraft, Inc., 1848 West 2300 South, Salt Lake City, Utah, 84119, except in the case of brief passages embodied in critical reviews and articles. Bookcraft is a registered trademark of Bookcraft, Inc.

Library of Congress Catalog Card Number: 88-71564

ISBN 0-88494-667-3

First Printing, 1988

Printed in the United States of America

And by the power of the Holy Ghost ye may know the truth of all things. (Moroni 10:5.)

And now, verily, verily, I say unto thee, put your trust in that Spirit which leadeth to do good—yea, to do justly, to walk humbly, to judge righteously; and this is my Spirit. Verily, verily, I say unto you, I will impart unto you of my Spirit, which shall enlighten your mind, which shall fill your soul with joy; and then shall ye know, or by this shall you know, all things whatsoever you desire of me, which are pertaining unto things of righteousness, in faith believing in me that you shall receive. (D&C 11:12–14.)

Contents

Prophets

1	The Need for Prophets	3
2	How Prophets Are Called	21
3	Prophets Foreknown	48
4	The Discerning of Prophets	69
5	That All Might Be Prophets	90

Prophecy

6	The Need for Prophecy	105
7	How Prophecy Comes	121
8	Scriptures Foreknown	141
9	The Discerning of Prophecy	155
10	That All Might Prophesy	171
	Bibliography	191
	Subject Index	197
	Scripture Index	209

Prophets

1

Surely the Lord God will do nothing, but he revealeth his secret unto his servants the prophets.
—Amos 3:7

The Need for Prophets

Were our modern day to produce a Moses—one claiming to have stood face to face with the Almighty—who among the throngs of this world would accept his claim? Among the Catholics, Protestants, Jews, or Muslims, all of whom profess an acceptance of the ancient Moses as a prophet, who would fail to willingly accept a modern successor? Surely the announcement that such a prophet again walked the earth could only be received with rejoicing among people of faith and goodness.

Though perhaps naturally skeptical of such an announcement, shouldn't we find ourselves hoping it to be true? Should not the very thought of a living prophet thrill the soul of every righteous man and woman? Surely a modern Moses could but enhance our love for and understanding of the ancient Moses. The spirit of a modern prophet could have no other effect than to bind and tie us more closely to his ancient counterparts. There was no impropriety in Elisha seeking a double portion of that spirit that had rested upon Elijah. Nor does the calling of Matthias to fill the vacancy in the meridian Twelve lessen our love for those who had already been called to that sacred office.

In his mortal ministry, Christ was profoundly respectful of the prophets who had preceded him. An avid student of the writings of the Old Testament prophets, he testified of their inspiration and admonished all to carefully study them. He also ordained and blessed others to lead his people after his death, telling them that they would do greater things than they had seen him do (John 14:12). It is a brotherhood that we sense among the prophets of all ages, not a rivalry. Christ honored the past prophets and called and ordained a new generation of prophets. In none of this was he demeaned; in all of it he was honored.

Ancient Prophets and Their Function

Perhaps the strongest argument for the necessity of prophets in modern times comes from understanding the function of prophets anciently. From the beginning of time God chose to bestow the treasures of eternity in "earthen vessels" (2 Corinthians 4:7). He elected to manifest his mind and will to us through men of "human frailties" (NEB, James 5:17), men "no less mortal" (NEB, Acts 14:15) than us all. Of Christ himself the scriptural record declares, "We have not an high priest which cannot be touched with the feelings of our infirmities," for "in all points" he was "tempted like as we are" (Hebrews 4:15). Whether it be to declare his mind, teach his doctrines, record his word, typify his presence in the performance of ritual, or lead his people, God has chosen the faltering voice of man, languages born in the day of Babel, and the pen of the untutored to represent him. Indeed, he has a propensity for choosing the weak and the simple as instruments by whom to manifest his knowledge and power.

It is the order of heaven to grant man and nations all they are willing and ready to receive. Alma stated the principle thus: "The Lord doth grant unto all nations, of their own nation and tongue, to teach his word, yea, in wisdom, all that he seeth fit that they should have" (Alma 29:8). Alma further assured us that "it is given unto many to know the mysteries of God; nevertheless they are laid under a strict command that they shall not impart only according to the portion of his word which he doth grant unto the children of men, according to the heed and diligence which they give unto him" (Alma 12:9). It is of these teachers, called and ordained of God, that we seek to learn. To do so, let us review their role as we find it described in the scriptures.

The Function of a Prophet in the Old Testament

The word *prophet* as found in the Old Testament comes from the Hebrew *nabi*. The original meaning of the root is not known. Scholars are in general agreement, however, that the lost Hebrew root is related to cognate Akkadian and Arabic words meaning "called" or "to call," conveying the idea that a prophet is one called of God, or meaning "to announce," or "to proclaim," emphasizing that a prophet is one who proclaims the will of God.[1] Usage has established the meaning. In the context of the Old Testament, a prophet (nabi) was one who had been called of God to be his spokesman.

The primary function of the Old Testament prophet is that of covenant spokesman. His role, as one authority noted, is essentially that of "exhortation, not mere prediction. While it is true that foretelling is an important ingredient and may serve as a sign of the prophet's authority (Deut. 18:22; Isa. 41:22; 43:9), his essential task is to declare the word of God to the here and now; to disclose the future in order to illumine what is involved in the present."[2]

The Old Testament contains more than three hundred references to prophets (nabim). They apply to a remarkable range of characters. Abraham is the first so named (Genesis 20:7), though Adam ought to be; Haggai is the last so identified (Haggai 2:1), though John the Baptist should be. Between these references the word is used to describe a colorful variety of personalities and their activities ranging from Aaron (Exodus 7:1) to Zechariah (Zechariah 1:7), from the waywardness of Jonah to the steadfastness of Isaiah, from the ethical Nathan to visionaries like Ezekiel and Daniel, from the objective perspective of Amos to the intensely involved Jeremiah, from the unwavering faith and obedience of Abraham to the perfidy of Balaam.

In early Old Testament times a prophet was called a seer, from the Hebrew *ro'eh*, meaning "one who sees" (1 Samuel 9:9). Contextually this carried the idea of seeing that which was hidden to others. The Hebrew *hozen*, meaning "one who sees a vision," also has been translated as "seer." In addition, *hozen* carries the meaning, "to tell," "to declare," or "to make known." Other descriptive names commonly associated with the prophetic office were "messenger" (Haggai 1:13), "watchman" (Hosea 9:8), "servant" (Amos 3:7), and "assayer [tester]" of the people (RSV, Jeremiah 6:27). Prophets were also closely associated with holy places or the performance of religious ritual, and in some instances held the office of priest. Some of the prophets were itinerants moving about with considerable freedom, and apparently were maintained by offerings from the Saints.

There were also presiding prophets—those who stood at the head of what scholars have described as "prophetic guilds." The scriptures simply refer to these groups as the "sons of the prophets" (1 Kings 20:35; 2 Kings 2:3, 5, 7, 15; 4:1, 38; 5:22; 6:1; 9:1). The mystery of their nature and function may find rather simple explanation in the announcement to our dispensation that those who are faithful in the obtaining of the Aaronic and Melchizedek Priesthoods and "the magnifying their calling . . . become the sons of Moses and of Aaron and the seed of Abraham" (D&C 84:33–34); that is, they become the "sons of the prophets." The apostasy being sufficiently general among ancient Israel during most periods of her history, it may have been necessary for the faithful brethren of the priesthood to band together in small societies of their own. It is noted that these prophets would often prophesy in groups (1 Samuel 10:5; 19:20), which was also a practice among the meridian Saints (1 Corinthians 14:29–31). It is generally conceded that the Old Testament prophets "wore a distinctive costume consisting of a hairy sheepskin or goatskin mantle and a leather loincloth"[3] (2 Kings 1:8; Zechariah 13:4). It also appears that there was a system of prophetic succession (2 Kings 2:9–15; Deuteronomy 3:21–22, 28; 34:9).

The Function of Prophets in the New Testament

Defining the function of prophets is a more manageable task when examining the New Testament than the Old. The writings of Paul and John indicate that all within the faith —both men and women—should be able to speak as prophets or prophetesses (Acts 2:16–18; 1 Corinthians 14:29–32; Revelation 19:10). It is a "widespread view" among New Testament scholars "that in early Christianity all Christians were potential, if not actual, prophets."[4] The commonalty of prophets among the congregations of the meridian Saints is seen in the frequent warnings against false prophets that would arise among their numbers (Matthew 7:15; 24:11; 2 Peter 2:1; 1 John 4:1). Though it was believed to be within the province of all to prophesy, some were specifically identified as holding the office of a prophet in the ecclesiastical hierarchy of the Church (see 1 Corinthians 12:28–29; Ephesians 2:19–20; 4:11). Thus, while it appears that the Saints in New Testament times took seriously Moses' injunction that all the Lord's people be prophets (Numbers 11:29), and each member of the congregation was expected to have the spirit of prophecy, being a prophet or a prophetess in his or her own right, certain of their number were ordained to the office and calling of a prophet or Apostle and thus were placed in a hierarchal position to give direction and leadership to the Church.

Since the New Testament comes to us from Greek manuscripts, we must turn to Greek to find the etymology of the word *prophet*. The Greek word *prophetes* (prophet) is the only word the New Testament uses to translate the Hebrew *nabi*. "In pagan Greek the term *prophetes* (feminine *prophetis*) had no necessary connection with revelatory activity and means simply 'spokesman' or 'announcer'; however, as a designation of the particular cultic official at Greek oracle sanctuaries who transmitted oracular responses to inquirers, the term took on the technical meaning 'one who speaks on behalf of the god.' " In its pagan usage *prophetes* "was never laden with such connotations as 'one who predicts the future' (the prefix *pro-* meant 'forth,' not 'fore') or 'inspired spokesman,' though it was given that meaning in Biblical Greek and in the literature of both early Judaism and early Christianity."[5]

Among the meridian Saints a prophet was the proclaimer of the divine message—to prophesy was to speak forth the mind of God. The role of the prophet in the New Testament was that of edifying, encouraging, and extending comfort (1 Corinthians 14:3). Prophets were able to predict future events (Acts 11:28; 21:10ff), know the past (John 4:18–19), and read the hearts of men (Luke 7:39), but their primary role was to teach the saving principles of the gospel of Jesus Christ. Thus the verb *to prophesy* was also used in reference to the proclamation of the divine message (1 Corinthians 11:4–5), to foretelling (Mark 7:6; Luke 1:67), to teaching, admonishing, and comforting (1 Corinthians 14:3, 31), and to glorifying God (Acts 10:44–47).

The Function of Prophets in the Book of Mormon

Among Book of Mormon peoples a prophet was understood to be a man "chosen of God" (Helaman 9:16) to speak his words (Alma 5:11). He was one to whom God had given great power and authority (Helaman 11:18) to act in his name (Alma 19:4). The Book of Mormon makes a clear distinction between a seer and a prophet. Ammon declares a seer to be greater than a prophet. By way of explanation he states: "A seer is a revelator and a prophet also; and a gift which is greater can no man have, except he should possess the power of God, which no man can; yet a man may have great power given him from God. But a seer can know of things which are past, and also of things which are to come, and by them shall all things be revealed, or, rather, shall secret things be made manifest, and hidden things shall come to light, and things which are not known shall be made known by them, and also things shall be made known by them which otherwise could not be known." (Mosiah 8:16–17.)

Ammon's definition is perfectly harmonious with what we have found in the Bible. He perceives the prophet as an inspired preacher of the mind and will of God, while the seer, who has an even greater gift, can envision the past, the present, and the future—the emphasis in both instances being that saving truths can only be known by the spirit of prophecy and revelation. As Ammon presents it, truth is the revealed knowledge of things as they are, the revealed knowledge of things as they were, and the revelation of things as they are to come. That which is more or less than this, that which has been obtained other than by the spirit of prophecy and revelation—having as its source some other spirit—is not of God (see D&C 93:24–25). It is fundamental to the message of the Book of Mormon that without the spirit of prophecy and revelation there can be no true religion (Mormon 9:7–21).

The Function of the Ancient Prophets

Elder Anthony W. Ivins states:

> A careful study of the etymology of the word and of the lives, works and character of the prophets of old makes clear the fact that a prophet was, and is, one called to act as God's messenger. He is to teach men the character of God, and define and make known to the people, his will. He is to denounce sin, and declare the punishment of transgression. He is to be above all else a preacher of righteousness, and when the people depart from the path which he has marked out for them to follow, is to call them back to the true faith. He is an interpreter of the scripture, and declares its meaning and application. When future events are to be declared he predicts them, but his direct and most important calling is to be a forth-teller, or director of present policy, rather than a foreteller of that which is to come.[6]

It ought be observed that a broad distinction exists between what in the primitive Church was known as "prophesying" and what in subsequent times has come to be known as "preaching." The fact that a fool preaches a sermon hardly argues that he is a prophet. Preaching is prophesying only when the preacher speaks by the power of the Holy Ghost, when what he says is the will, mind, and word of the

Lord (D&C 68:4). Should the ordained prophet preach without the authority of the Holy Ghost he has not spoken as a prophet.

No prophecy ever came by the will of man, Peter declared, "but holy men of God spake as they were moved by the Holy Ghost" (2 Peter 1:21). The apostasy that followed the meridian day saw rhetoric supplant the spontaneous direction of the spirit of revelation. It centered in a message crafted for public acceptance. The true prophet, in contrast, seeks no say in the message. He does not curry favor. His message, as Jeremiah said, will not be one of peace or of self-gratification (Jeremiah 23:17). His will not be a practiced delivery; he will not have honed homiletic skills. His power will be in the Spirit. He will come, as did Paul, without "excellency of speech or wisdom, declaring . . . the testimony of God" (1 Corinthians 2:1). He will not be applauded, nor will he be paid.

In our day preachers imitate the form of prophecy but are without the substance. They set forth "truths of utterance rather than truths of their lives." Edwin Hatch, in his masterful work *The Influence of Greek Ideas on Christianity*, observed that modern Christianity tries "to make the echo of the past sound like the voice of the present." The religion of the New Testament, he observed, "came into the educated world in the simple dress of a Prophet of Righteousness. It won that world by the stern reality of its life, by the subtle bonds of its brotherhood, by its divine message of consolation and of hope. Around it thronged the race of eloquent talkers who persuaded it to change its dress and to assimilate its language to their own. It seemed thereby to win a speedier and completer victory. But it purchased conquest at the price of reality. With that its progress stopped."[7]

Thus prophesying gave way to preaching and preaching to priestcraft. It was as Paul had prophesied—a time when men would not endure sound doctrine, for they fed their own lusts and heaped to themselves teachers, having itching ears (2 Timothy 4:3).

The Law of Witnesses Requires Prophets

*People of All Ages Are Entitled to Be
Taught the Gospel by Competent Witnesses*

The justice of God requires that all people be granted adequate opportunity to hear and receive the gospel message. One could hardly be held accountable for rejecting the plan of salvation having not heard it, or having heard it taught only by uninformed or incompetent teachers. Surely the heavens cannot ratify such efforts. We cannot teach what we do not understand, nor can we testify of that which we have not experienced. To those of our day the Lord has said, "If ye receive not the Spirit ye shall not teach" (D&C 42:14). Paul taught the same principle, saying, "For what man knoweth the things of a man, save the spirit of man which is in him? even so the things of God knoweth no man, but the Spirit of God" (1 Corinthians 2:11). There are standards with which the teaching of the gospel must comply if its message is to be binding on those to whom it has been taught.

The heavenly ordained system to assure that the gospel is properly taught is known to us as the law of witnesses. Witnesses specially chosen of God are endowed with a sure and perfect knowledge of God and those principles essential to salvation. By the power of the Spirit they in turn teach and testify of these principles to those of their generation. Never in scriptural writ does a prophet or Apostle pretend that the revelation given to his predecessors makes him a special witness. Each has been individually called and personally endowed with his message and authority. Such has been the common lot of prophets in all ages.

Such being the order of heaven in all past dispensations, we can suppose that it is equally essential in our day. Either there are competent witnesses—those who have obtained their message and their commission from God himself—and their witness has been made known to us, or we are free from the obligation to accept and live gospel principles. Plainly stated, without living prophets there is no gospel and never has been. The gospel is not a book. A person does not profess to have law because he possesses a law book, or music because he has a musical score. Similarly, no valid profession can be made to having the gospel because one possesses a Bible or some other book of scripture. To have the gospel one must have the Holy Ghost; and since the Holy Ghost is a revelator, one cannot have the Holy Ghost without having revelation; and one cannot claim revelation without claiming prophets.

There Can Be No Authoritative Declaration of the Gospel Without Prophets

The Gospel Is Acquired Only by Revelation

As to the doctrines of salvation, they are not of man's making, nor of his choosing—they are not the offspring of scholarship, the creations of earthly governments, or the masterwork of intellectuals. There are not many Lords, many faiths, and many baptisms, nor are there alternate plans of salvation. We have not been invited to choose from among the commandments of God to determine our own system of worship. Ignorance, even when innocent, does not exalt man, and sincerity in a false cause is a dangerous predator of truth. Only heaven-sent truths in companionship with righteousness and obedience can guide us up the narrow path of Mount Zion to the place of the divine presence.

In God's plan there is to be no uncertainty among men as to what are the principles of salvation. If the doctrines of salvation were a matter of opinion, if all roads led to Rome, as LDS missionaries are so often told, there would be no need for Christ, nor his prophets in any age. Indeed, then there could be no false prophets, or false Christs, or false doctrines; distinction between truth and error would be needless, and all would be free to concoct their own systems of worship, announce their own requirements for salvation, and devise their own kingdoms of glory. Sincerity and goodness would, of course, be proclaimed as the god of salvation, and all men would be left to decide the proper place of each in their lives. The glory of such a system would be that none would be lost, no matter how wicked their lives appeared in the eyes of others. As his own judge, each could exalt himself. Such would be our circumstance unless God, with sufficient clarity for all to understand, announced otherwise — and so, the heavens be praised, he has done!

Christ Set a Timeless Example

From time immemorial the heavenly ordained system whereby men might know with perfect assurance the path they are to follow has been to declare the gospel through the instrumentality of living prophets. The ministry of Christ constitutes the perfect example of the manner in which the gospel is to be taught in all ages. If the system of heaven was that men feast on the words of a heaven-sent book, and that book alone, it would have been most fitting for Christ in his ministry to conform to the pattern, presenting the book and confining himself to it. Quite to the contrary, Christ freely added to the sacred writings of the past, called and commissioned many to be personal witnesses of him, and promised the gift of revelation to all who would faithfully accept their testimony. What Christ did in his ministry was to multiply prophets and prophecy. In so doing he indicated in both word and deed that this ought ever be the order of things.

There Can Be No Ambiguity About the Principles of Salvation

God is not the author of uncertainty, confusion, division, or contention. The necessity of baptism cannot be in question. The need for repentance is not open to debate. The question of who can hold the priesthood is not to be decided by popular vote. Saving principles are not determined by governmental pressures. Servants of God are not chosen on the basis of their power and influence among men. Heaven's blessings are not marketed and sold. The Church of God must in all ages be both a "true" and a "living" church. It must have within it those who, having personally received their errand from the Lord, can speak with authority.

Prophets Are Necessary for the Exercise of Priesthood

There is an inseparable link between prophets and priesthood. To profess to hold the priesthood of God is to claim that one is an authorized representative of the Lord. Priesthood is the authority to represent God in the teaching of his gospel and the performance of the ordinances of salvation as he instituted them. To profess priesthood on the one hand and deny the principles of revelation on the other is a contradiction in terms. How, might we ask, does a God who cannot speak go about appointing or commissioning agents to represent him? And were one to claim a commission from this non-speaking God, how would he ever obtain the assurance that what he was doing met with God's approval? Further still, without revelation how would those over whom this priesthood holder was to preside ascertain that his claim to authority was to be respected and trusted?

True, it has been argued that priesthood comes from the Bible or from the faith of the believers. Yet the Bible sustains no such claim, and a priesthood born of "belief" could easily become a commission to perpetrate all manner of mischief. Arguments are also made for a priesthood that traces itself back to the ministry of Christ needing only the original revelation that gave it. Such a priesthood has little resemblance to that from which it professes to come—for the priesthood of Christ and the Apostles was a priesthood of revelation, miracles, and all manner of heavenly power. Can it be the same priesthood if it cannot claim the same powers?

There is no priesthood unless there are prophets, for the spirit of revelation is the very life blood of that authority by which men are authorized to represent God. Prophets and priesthood are indeed inseparable—for priesthood cannot properly be used independent of the spirit of prophecy and revelation. To properly exercise priesthood is to stand in the stead of God, saying what he would say, and doing what he would do—such is the very spirit of prophecy.

Prophets Are a Legacy of the Righteous

What circumstances existed anciently that prevailed upon the heavens to send prophets that do not exist today? Is there not sufficient wickedness to merit raising the warning voice? Is there not sufficient confusion even in the general Christian world to warrant a clear dictum from the heavens? And what of the honest truth-seekers—those willing to follow prophets—ought they not to have prophets to follow? Some argue that the writings of the ancient Apostles and prophets are sufficient to lead today's church. Yet no one would argue that a library containing the memoirs of great generals fills the need for generals in today's armies. Great books may instruct and inspire those who would be leaders, but they will never replace those leaders. Just as the strategy and courage of dead warriors will not win today's battles, the faith and repentance of the meridian Saints will not remit our sins. History wields no sword. The courage of those now dead will win no battles. Even righteous history can swear no allegiance to one cause over another. For that matter, the Bible has all too often been a conscripted slave in wicked causes.

It was neither history nor tradition that fired the bones of the faithful in Bible days. As the righteous of that day laid claim to the powers of heaven, so the righteous of our day must have equal claim to those same powers. If God, who is the same yesterday, today, and forever, gave *them* priesthood and power, he must in justice give *us* priesthood and power; if he gave *them* prophets and revelation, he must in justice give *us* the same. Our battle is not less than theirs. Satan as well as God is the same yesterday, today, and forever. He still commissions prophets to represent him in leading his knights of darkness. Can the God of heaven do less?

Prophets Are the Constitution of the Church

The constitution of the kingdom of God is not a document. The authority by which the Church operates is not claimed from scrolls of parchment pieced together by zealous scholars, nor is it found in revelations given even in our own day. If it be a "true and living church," it must have a true and living constitution, and so it has. Acting through his prophets, God is our constitution, and his word our law. As to earthly matters, God has ordained prophets, seers, and revelators to represent him in this day, as he has ever done. The united voice of those prophets as they are directed by the spirit of prophecy and revelation is the constitution of the Church and kingdom of God on earth. One among their number is chosen to stand at the head and the others willingly follow, for their purpose is the same and the Lord's house is a house of order. Paul declared the principle, stating that "the spirits of the prophets are subject to the prophets" (1 Corinthians 14:32), meaning that truth is always in harmony with itself and that this same unity will exist among the servants of truth.

On one occasion Joseph Smith gave a committee headed by John Taylor the assignment of writing a constitution for the Kingdom of God. The committee's labors were futile, and they so reported to the Prophet Joseph. He matter-of-factly acknowledged their failure, stating that "they could not draft a constitution worthy of guiding the Kingdom of God" and that he had gone before the Lord seeking that such a constitution be granted by revelation. In response to his entreaties the Lord said: "*Ye are my constitution* and I am your God and ye are my spokesman, therefore from henceforth keep my commandments."[8] No book will ever be able to replace the need for the spirit of revelation. How foolish to suppose that the wisdom of God can be confined to a written document or even a volume of scripture!

The Writings of Dead Prophets Cannot Direct a Living Church

As Latter-day Saints we quote from, expound, teach from, and glory in the Bible, but it is not the source of our doctrine or our hope of salvation. No people believe it more devoutly than we do; none attempt to learn its truths and live its laws more diligently. We cannot speak too highly or say too much that is good and supportive of the ancient holy scriptures. But the Bible is not the source of doctrine in this day; it is but a supplemental witness; it is a source of added knowledge about those things that have been given us by direct revelation. When we go forth to teach the doctrines of salvation, our commission (and it is a commandment to us) is to teach the revelations and commandments that have come to us through the Prophet Joseph Smith.

To those of this dispensation the Lord has said: "Your minds in times past have been darkened because of unbelief, and because you have treated lightly the things you have received—which vanity and unbelief have brought the whole church under condemnation." In that spirit of unbelief we have treated lightly the First Vision, the Book of Mormon, the revealed word as it has come by latter-day revelation. There has been a tendency to turn to the Bible in seeking justification for our doctrines, rather than glorying in the words of the prophets who came in our day to bring the word of salvation to us. "And this condemnation resteth upon the children of Zion, even all. And they shall remain under this condemnation until they repent and remember the new covenant, even the Book of Mormon and the former commandments which I have given them, not only to say, but to do according to that which I have written." (D&C 84:54–57.) The word of the Lord to us is to use the Book of Mormon and the revelations given through Joseph Smith as the source of our gospel knowledge.

The Bible is what the Bible is, but the word of salvation to us comes from the prophet sent to minister as the head of our dispensation. To those who follow this course the Lord has said: "I will forgive you of your sins with this commandment—that you remain steadfast in your minds in solemnity and the spirit of prayer, in bearing testimony to all the world of those things which are communicated unto you" (D&C 84:61). "Those things which [have been] communicated unto" us take precedence over all other revealed truth, no matter what its source. Thus our attention is properly centered in the message of the restoration.

People of All Ages Are Required to Accept the Prophet Sent in Their Day and Age

Men need always to look to the prophets sent to them. They cannot fondly gaze back to former days and expect thereby to gain the blessings of heaven. There are two obvious reasons for this. First, all men are entitled to hear the eternal word taught in plainness and purity as it applies to the particular cultural, social, and religious circumstances in which they live. It was one thing for Paul to preach to people who believed in and served under a corrupted version of the law of Moses. It is quite another thing for Joseph Smith to preach to people who have believed in and served under a corrupted Christianity. The second reason why people need to look to the prophets and Apostles sent to them is that only legal administrators can validly perform the ordinances of salvation. Those seeking such ordinances must find those who are endowed with power from on high, who hold the holy priesthood, who truly represent the Lord, who have power to bind on earth and have that binding sealed eternally in the heavens.

Without Prophets There Is No Gospel

Declared Joseph Smith:

> If any person should ask me if I were a prophet, I should not deny it, as that would give me the lie; for, according to John, the testimony of Jesus is the spirit of prophecy; therefore, if I profess to be a witness or teacher, and have not the spirit of prophecy, which is the testimony of Jesus, I must be a false witness; but if I be a true teacher and witness, I must possess the spirit of prophecy, and that constitutes a prophet; and any man who says he is a teacher or a preacher of righteousness, and denies the spirit of prophecy, is a liar, and the truth is not in him; and by this key false teachers and impostors may be detected.[9]

In a conversation with a judge in 1843 Joseph Smith explained that he "did not profess to be a prophet any more than every man ought to who professes to be a preacher of righteousness; and that the testimony of Jesus is the spirit of prophecy."[10]

Conclusions

1. The religion proclaimed by the Bible is not the result of man's search for God; rather, it is an account of God manifesting himself to man. That is to say, the religion of the Bible is always revealed religion, a religion declared only by those called by God and ordained to speak in his behalf. Never is it a system of theology concocted by the councils and schools of men. Nor was it ever a religion dependent on tradition as a source of authority. It has been insightfully observed that "it is impossible for any one, whether he be a student of history or no, to fail to notice a difference of both form and content between the Sermon on the Mount and the Nicene Creed. . . . The one belongs to a world of Syrian peasants, the other to a world of Greek philosophers."[11]

2. Prophets and prophecy are and ever have been the mark of true religion. In all of scriptural writ the Lord never had a people to whom he did not give prophets. "Surely the Lord God will do nothing," Amos declared, "but he revealeth his secret unto his servants the prophets" (Amos 3:7). Ancient prophets stood as the link between God and men. Their voice became his voice, their words his words, their pen his pen. He manifested his mind and will through them. He evidenced his power through them, and he led and guided his people through them. They were inspired teachers of the gospel, and they were entrusted with the authority to perform the ordinances of salvation. They were the source of inspired teaching; they marked the path the Saints were to follow. To be without prophets is to be without the gospel, without priesthood, without the light of heaven, and without the plan of salvation. If we have need for a living God, we have need for living prophets.

Notes

1. Napier, "Prophet, Prophetism," *The Interpreter's Dictionary of the Bible*, 3:896-97; Kittel and Friedrich, *Theological Dictionary of the New Testament*, p. 954.

In Hebrew the verbal root of *nabi* means to "bubble" or "spring forth." Used in the form of a noun it means one in whom the message of God springs forth, or one to whom anything is secretly communicated. (Harris, Archer, and Waltke, *Theological Wordbook of the Old Testament*, 2:544; Smith, *A Dictionary of the Bible*, p. 534.)

2. Heschel, *The Prophets*, 1:12.
3. Aune, *Prophecy in Early Christianity and the Ancient Mediterranean World*, p. 83.
4. Aune, *Prophecy in Early Christianity*, p. 195.
5. Aune, *Prophecy in Early Christianity*, p. 195.
6. Ivins, Conference Report, October 1925, p. 20.
7. Hatch, *The Influence of Greek Ideas on Christianity*, p. 114.
8. Joseph F. Smith, Minutes of the Council of Fifty, April 21, 1880; cited in Millet, "The Development of the Concept of Zion in Mormon Theology," pp. 169–70.
9. Joseph Smith, Jr., *Teachings of the Prophet Joseph Smith*, p. 269; hereafter cited as *Teachings*.
10. Joseph Smith, Jr., *History of the Church*, 5:231–32.
11. Hatch, *The Influence of Greek Ideas on Christianity*, p. 1.

2

"Ye have not chosen me, but I have chosen you, and ordained you, that ye should go and bring forth fruit.
—John 15:16

How Prophets Are Called

It is for God to choose his own messengers—doing so in such a manner that the honest in heart can and will recognize them as such. Christ provides the pattern—after a night's prayer, in which he sought the revelation of heaven, he chose those intimate associates who would surround him in his earthly ministry and be the special witnesses of his name and gospel in all the world. To them, twelve in number, he said: "Ye have not chosen me, but I have chosen you, and ordained you, that ye should go and bring forth fruit, and that your fruit should remain: that whatsoever ye shall ask of the Father in my name, he may give it to you" (John 15:16). Christ designated them "apostles" (Luke 6:13), the literal meaning of which is "one sent forth" (*apo*, "forth," and *stello*, "to send"). Inherent to the word *apostle* is the idea of a commission and the further thought of authorization.[1] Of themselves the Apostles had no authority and espoused no doctrines. These divinely sent teachers professed authority only in the name of Christ and only on his errand. Yet that authority was plenipotentiary—they professed to bind on earth and bind in heaven, or to loose on earth and loose in heaven (see Matthew 16:19; John 20:13). As to doctrines, they echoed the teachings of their Master, promising exaltation in their acceptance and damnation in their rejection.

For that day when Christ would leave them, they were given the assurance of continual direction by revelation (see John 15:26; 16:7–13).

Restoration of the Prophetic Office

The restoration of the prophetic office demands the opening of the heavens. One could hardly profess to be God's spokesman for a dispensation and at the same time profess a God who does not speak. The voice of God must be more than a distant echo from the Judean hills; it must be more than the record of what inspired men once said and once did. The cleansing power of John's baptism in the waters of Jordan was not intended to wash away the sins of all future generations any more than the fish and the loaves miraculously provided by the Savior would satisfy their hunger. "Our gospel came not unto you in word only," the Apostle Paul reminded the ancient Saints, "but also in power, and in the Holy Ghost, and in much assurance" (1 Thessalonians 1:5). The gospel is a living thing, the performance of its ordinances demands living officiators; the declaration of its truths demands a living voice—spokesmen who know whereof they speak, having heard that voice for themselves. No prophetic voice within the covers of holy writ has been solely dependent on what God said to others, nor has one such ever suggested that he would be the last of the prophets.

The house of God has always been a house of order. What then is the system ordained in the heavens whereby the gospel is to be declared to the nations of the earth? As restored in this dispensation, we know the following:

The Lord chose his spokesmen even before they were born. Joseph Smith declared this principle thus: "Every man who has a calling to minister to the inhabitants of the world was ordained to that very purpose in the Grand Council of heaven before this world was."[2] Of himself he said that the cause of his persecutions "seems mysterious, unless I was ordained from before the foundation of the world for some good end, or bad, as you may choose to call it. Judge ye for yourselves." (D&C 127:2.) In translating the Book of Mormon he learned that those ordained to the higher or Melchizedek Priesthood were "called and prepared from the foundation of the world according to the foreknowledge of God, on account of their exceeding faith and good works" in their first estate. Others, those not called, forfeited that privilege because of the "hardness of their hearts and blindness of their minds, while if it had not been for this they might have had as great privilege as their brethren." (Alma 13:3–6.)

None have the authority to represent God save he calls them. "It shall not be given to any one to go forth to preach my gospel," the Lord declared as he laid the foundations of the Restoration, "or to build up my church, except he be ordained by someone who has authority, and it is known to the church that he has authority and has been regularly ordained by the heads of the church" (D&C 42:11). Similarly, Joseph Smith wrote: "A man must be called of God, by prophecy, and by the laying on of hands by those who are in authority, to preach the Gospel and administer in the ordinances thereof" (Articles of Faith 1:5).

All gospel principles claim revelation as their source. As the messenger must be called of God, so the message must be the manifestation of God's mind and will. Speaking to Joseph Smith, the Lord said: "This generation shall have my word through you" (D&C 5:10); to all others the direction is "you shall declare the things which have been revealed to my servant, Joseph Smith, Jun." (D&C 31:4). As the meridian Twelve were to echo the teachings of the Master, so those properly commissioned in our day proclaim those things restored to our dispensation head (see D&C 1:18). "Preach my gospel," the Lord said, "which ye have received, even as ye have received it" (D&C 49:1).

The true messenger must be true to the message. We have been promised the sustaining power of heaven when we teach the revelations of the Restoration; when we do otherwise, the Lord said, we will not prosper (see D&C 49:4).

"With some I am not well pleased," the Lord said of early missionaries of this dispensation, "for they will not open their mouths, but they hide the talent which I have given unto them, because of the fear of man. Wo unto such, for mine anger is kindled against them. And it shall come to pass, if they are not more faithful unto me, it shall be taken away, even that which they have." (D&C 60:2–3.) Because he bowed to the "persuasions of men," the youthful Joseph Smith lost the privilege of translation for a time and season (D&C 3:6–8).

Those properly commissioned of God are endowed with power from on high. As the Apostles of the meridian day went forth clothed in the powers of heaven, with the promise of divine protection to preach the gospel, and as they had power to heal the sick, raise the dead, remit sins, and perform all manner of miracles, so those of our day must go forth. "Ye are to be taught from on high," the Lord said. Therefore "sanctify yourselves and ye shall be endowed with power, that ye may give even as I have spoken" (D&C 43:16; compare 95:8–9). That his servants might go forth armed with power, that his name might be upon them, that his glory might be round about them, and that his angels might have charge over them, temples have been built wherein special blessings and powers are granted (see D&C 109:21–22).

The prophet and his message must stand independent of the world. True religion must stand independent of the power and influences of the world. Mormonism professes no authority, power, keys, or doctrines for which it is dependent or indebted to any people on earth. All that we profess, we profess by divine revelation. Our priesthoods, our doctrines, our ordinances have all been given to us by messengers from heaven. We need not hide behind Bible texts. We have what we have because God has spoken directly to us, because messengers from his presence have brought us authority they received at his hand, because the doctrine, faith, and power of which the Bible speaks has been given to us anew. As the faithful of ages past had their gospel dispensations, so we have ours.

Old Testament: Calling of Prophets

From Joseph Smith's statement on the subject given earlier in this chapter it is clear that every prophet of every dispensation received his call to that office in the premortal life and was foreordained to it in the Grand Council in heaven. In most cases scripture does not contain sufficient detail for us to determine when and how the call came in mortality, though Joseph Smith made clear their priesthood authority: "All the prophets had the Melchizedek Priesthood."[3] Frequently, (as with Hosea, Joel, Jonah, Micah, Zephaniah, Haggai, and Zechariah) the prophet's first expression as it has come down to us is that "the word of the Lord came unto" him, but the manner of its coming, and whether it constituted his earthly call as a prophet or even was the first message he received from the divine source, is not explained.

> The Lord has various means of communicating with a prophet, but they may all be encompassed by a King James Version rendering of an expression by Jeremiah. In chapter 23 he recounts the Lord's strictures on the false prophets who preface their lies with "The Lord hath said," and the Lord's condemnation that they did not represent him because they had not "stood in the counsel of the Lord" (Jeremiah 23:18, 22). By whatever means they received it, only that counsel could so inform, inspire, and authorize a man as to make him a true prophet of the Lord. In that sense, of course, Jeremiah's account represents a test of a prophet for all gospel dispensations. . . .
>
> The Lord's broad spectrum of available communication methods range from his voice coming into the mind, as with Enos (Enos 1:10), all the way to the visions and manifestations granted to seers such as Enoch (Moses 7) or Joseph Smith (D&C 137). Indeed, it seems it is the powers of seership that are brought into play in many of the outstanding revelations the scriptures record. . . .
>
> While the record does not suggest that such glorious visual experiences are vouchsafed to all prophets,

apparently they are given to those whose caliber, calling, and circumstances warrant it. This would particularly be the case for those heading gospel dispensations or those bringing critical messages, as to preexilic Israel.

[To certain situations of this kind it may be possible to] apply an alternate rendition of the Jeremiah statement previously referred to. As rendered in the King James Version, Jeremiah reports the Lord as asking: "For who hath stood in the counsel of the Lord, and hath perceived and heard his word? who hath marked his word, and heard it?" He then gives further words of the Lord as: "I have not sent these prophets, yet they ran: I have not spoken to them, yet they prophesied. But if they had stood in my counsel, and had caused my people to hear my words, then they should have turned them from their evil way, and from the evil of their doings." (Jeremiah 23:18, 21–22.)

The word *counsel* in these verses, meaning "to advise" or "to warn," has been replaced in our more recent Bible translations by the word *council*, which has reference to a "body" or an "assembly." The root word is the Hebrew *sod*, which carries with it the idea of an intimate council or assembly. On the basis of this interpretation and several apocryphal Old Testament texts, it may be that Jeremiah was referring to a heavenly council or assembly, his standard for the truths of salvation being that they must all trace back to the heavenly council presided over by God himself. (It is noted that in Amos's declaration "Surely the Lord God will do nothing, but he revealeth his secret unto his servants the prophets"—Amos 3:7—the word *secret* also is a translation of the Hebrew *sod* and carries the same meaning as the word *council* in the Jeremiah text above.) Legitimate prophets must have received their mission in the premortal heavenly council (see Abraham 3:22–23; *Teachings*, p. 365). Some too appear to have had that mission reiterated, and a specific commission given, in a heavenly council to which they were carried in a vision while they were in mortality.[4]

Isaiah. The great vision accorded to Isaiah (chapter 6) took place "in the year that king Uzziah died," though it would seem that the prophet may have been acting in that calling before that time (2 Chronicles 26:22; Isaiah 1:1). From his account it appears that in vision Isaiah stood in the presence of the Lord, who was sitting upon a throne surrounded by heavenly beings. Knowing that no unclean thing can enter the presence of the Lord without being destroyed, Isaiah's first concern was with his own worthiness. "Woe is me!" he said, "for I am undone; because I am a man of unclean lips, and I dwell in the midst of a people of unclean lips" (Isaiah 6:5). In response an angel of the Lord took a live coal off the altar and laid it upon Isaiah's mouth, saying, "Lo, this hath touched thy lips; and thine iniquity is taken away, and thy sin purged" (Isaiah 6:7). Isaiah then heard the Lord ask, relative to the message that needed to be taken to the house of Israel, "Whom shall I send, and who will go for us?" Realizing why he had been called to witness these events, Isaiah responded, "Here am I; send me" (Isaiah 6:8).

Isaiah was then charged to carry the Lord's word to His people, even though that people, being hard-hearted, would be without eyes to see or ears to hear his message (JST, Isaiah 6:9–10). In response to his question as to how long it would take before his people would understand his words, the Lord said that it would not be until after Judah had been destroyed, her inhabitants scattered, and a remnant gathered (Isaiah 6:11–13).

Ezekiel. Ezekiel had a similar visionary experience, in which he saw the glory of God on his throne. Overwhelmed by the occasion, the prophet fell upon his face. He then heard a voice telling him to stand upon his feet, and was filled with the Spirit as the Lord directed him, saying: "I send thee to the children of Israel, to a rebellious nation that hath rebelled against me: they and their fathers have transgressed against me, even unto this very day. For they are impudent children and stiffhearted. I do send thee unto them; and thou shalt say unto them, Thus saith the Lord

God. And they, whether they will hear or whether they will forbear, . . . shall know that there hath been a prophet among them." (Ezekiel 1:26–28; 2:1–5.)

Then came the admonition—be without fear, "though briers and thorns be with thee, and thou dost dwell among scorpions," speak the words of the Lord, and be not rebellious (Ezekiel 2:6–8). As to his message, Ezekiel symbolically received it by eating a book (Ezekiel 2:9–10; 3:1–3).

Jeremiah. To Jeremiah the Lord said: "Before I formed thee in the belly I knew thee; and before thou camest forth out of the womb I sanctified thee, and I ordained thee a prophet unto the nations" (Jeremiah 1:4–5). The passage is an affirmation of premortal life, of that estate being one of preparation and training, and that some were set apart and foreordained in that first estate to be the Lord's agents on earth.

Overwhelmed with a sense of inadequacy, Jeremiah sought relief from such responsibility, arguing that he was young and inarticulate. The Lord rejected his excuses, saying "I shall send thee, and whatsoever I command thee thou shalt speak." Jeremiah was then admonished that he was not to fear the faces of men, and the Lord reached forth and touched his mouth saying "I have put my words in thy mouth." As to the bounds of his mission, the Lord said: "I have this day set thee over the nations and over the kingdoms, to root out, and to pull down, and to destroy, and to throw down, to build, and to plant." (Jeremiah 1:6–10.)

Moses. Moses' call to the apostleship[5] came to him on the "mountain of God" (Exodus 3:1; 4:27; 18:5), or Horeb. It being "holy ground," Moses was required to remove his shoes (Exodus 3:5). Old Testament texts clearly establish Sinai or Horeb as a "sanctuary" or temple (Exodus 15:17). The Psalmist described God's bringing the children of Israel to Sinai, saying: "He brought them to the border of his sanctuary, even to this mountain, which his right hand had purchased" (Psalm 78:54). The King James text tells us that here the "angel of the Lord appeared unto him in a flame of fire out of the midst of a bush" (Exodus 3:2). The Joseph Smith

Translation is more explicit, stating that it was "the Lord" with whom Moses conversed.[6] In this dramatic theophany Moses was commissioned to lead the children of Israel out of their Egyptian bondage, to testify of the God of their fathers, and to bring them to worship God upon the holy mountain (Exodus 3:10, 12, 13–15).

No reference is made in the Exodus account to Moses' receiving either priesthood or its directing authority, the keys. By modern revelation we know that he received the Melchizedek Priesthood from his father-in-law, Jethro, and that this priesthood could be traced back to Adam, who in turn received it from God himself (D&C 84:6–16).[7] As to the keys or the right to preside over the gathering of Israel, there is no question that Moses held them, for he was called on to bestow those very keys upon Peter, James, and John in the presence of the Messiah on the Mount of Transfiguration,[8] and upon Joseph Smith and Oliver Cowdery in our dispensation (D&C 110:11). Moses being the first to preside over the gathering of the nation of Israel, it seems a reasonable assumption that he received the keys to do so from God as a part of his experience on Sinai.

Old Testament Prophets: Characteristics of the Call

In the prophetic calls given to Moses, Isaiah, and Ezekiel there is a discernible pattern. It embraces the following:

High mountain or "heavenly council" experience. Isaiah and Ezekiel each received a vision or manifestation in which he was a participant in a "heavenly council"—either as a new experience or as a "rerun" of the original premortal council in heaven. Moses received his commission direct from the Lord on a mountain.

Designation as an Apostle or sent one. Each prophet was formally called or "sent"; none came in the prophetic office of his own choosing.

Commissioned. Each was given his message and mission.

That is, the message he was to bear was specifically given him. It was not his prerogative to modify it in any way.

Admonition. As necessary, there was a formula of admonition that emphasized the difficulty of the office and gave assurances of divine support: "Be not afraid of them, neither be afraid of their words, though briers and thorns be with thee, and thou dost dwell among scorpions" (Ezekiel 2:6). "Certainly I will be with thee" (Exodus 3:12).

It is in such a context that the "sent one" received his mission and commission and was then appropriately admonished. A Jewish scholar summarized as follows an exhaustive study of the "ascension" or "heavenly council" theme as found in Mesopotamian literature: "In the Mesopotamian texts, the heavenly ascent is made by the king who is both wise scribe and visionary seer and is described as 'the Sent One.' The various aspects of this theme can be summarized as follows:

1. Ascent to heaven
2. Entering the heavenly place
3. Reception by the high god in his assembly
4. Purification
5. Anointing
6. Robing in royal or heavenly garments
7. Handing over the heavenly book or heavenly tablets to the bearer of revelation
8. Calling with names of honor
9. Initiation into the heavenly secrets
10. Enthronement on the god-father's throne
11. Sending forth with a commission or a message to instruct the generation"[9]

Revealed commentary on the Old Testament. If indeed Jeremiah intended his words to establish the necessity of those professing to be prophets tracing their message and commission to a heavenly council, and given that the only reference we have of his having had such an experience is that which took place in a premortal council, we conclude that that experience is sufficient to comply with his test. From what we can learn from the scriptures and from what we have been taught by Joseph Smith, we can confidently say that all true prophets and ministers of the gospel were called and ordained in the councils of heaven prior to the creation of the earth. At least some of their number have had the experience of witnessing the details of those events in vision, Abraham being an example (see Abraham 3:22–23).

Since we live in the dispensation of the fulness of times —that is, the dispensation in which all the authority and knowledge of the ancients is destined to be restored—Latter-day Saints have already had revealed to them a considerable amount of knowledge dealing with the office and call of the ancient prophets. While expanding on the scriptural and historical characteristics suggested in what we have already reviewed, these revelations comply with the ancient characteristics too perfectly to be a matter of chance. Let us briefly review the knowledge available to us from these sources.

High mountain or "heavenly council." The first chapter of the book of Moses is a restoration of an ancient scriptural text recounting remarkable spiritual experiences granted to Moses some time after his call on Sinai, yet prior to the Exodus (Moses 1:17, 25). The account begins with nothing less than Moses being "caught up into an exceedingly high mountain," where he talked to God face to face. In recounting the story, Moses takes particular pains to emphasize the necessity of his being clothed in the glory of God in order to endure the Lord's presence. "Now mine own eyes have beheld God," Moses said of the experience, "but not my natural, but my spiritual eyes, for my natural eyes could not have beheld; for I should have withered and died in his presence; but his glory was upon me; and I beheld his face, for I was transfigured before him" (Moses 1:2, 11). Joseph Smith, though not at the time conscious of doing so, here provided us with the proper story about Moses in the proper setting. Thus, as far as available scriptural texts are concerned, we can unquestionably establish Moses' prophetic calling.

A second contribution of the book of Moses is the marvelous amount of material that it restores to us about Enoch. Reference to Enoch in the Old Testament is relegated to a single sentence (see Genesis 5:21–24). In contrast, the book of Moses and the Doctrine and Covenants combine in more than a hundred and twenty verses to tell us of this remarkable prophet. Included in these revelations is the recitation of his call to the ministry. Enoch, we are told, "was twenty-five years old when he was ordained under the hand of Adam; and he was sixty-five and Adam blessed him" (D&C 107:48). As he journeyed in the land, Enoch "heard a voice from heaven" directing him to prophesy and declare repentance to the people of his day (Moses 6:27). Like Jeremiah, he professed to be "but a lad," and like Moses he attempted to excuse himself from the call on the grounds of ineptitude of speech, excuses that to the Lord were as foam upon the ocean waves (Moses 6:31). Subsequently, while Enoch was journeying from the land of Cainan he beheld a vision in which the heavens were opened to him and the Lord spoke to him (Moses 6:42). Again, while in prayer Enoch heard the voice of the Lord, this time directing him to go to the mount Simeon. "I turned and went up on the mount," Enoch said, "and as I stood upon the mount, I beheld the heavens open, and I was clothed upon with glory; and I saw the Lord; and he stood before my face, and he talked with me, even as a man talketh one with another, face to face; and he said unto me: Look, and I will show unto thee the world for the space of many generations." Whereupon Enoch was shown those future generations (Moses 7:3–4).

The idea that Enoch had the high mountain experience, as did Moses and others of the ancient prophets, is affirmed in apocryphal writings which have been found since Joseph Smith penned the verses just considered. For instance, Secrets of Enoch gives an account of Enoch being taken into the presence of the Lord. In this instance Michael is directed by the Lord to extract Enoch from out of his earthly clothes and anoint him with "delightful oil" and put him into the clothes of God's glory. This having been done, Enoch is quoted as saying, "I gazed at myself, and I had become like one of the glorious ones."[10] In another Enoch manuscript an account is given of Enoch's being taken again into the heavenly court, clothed with the garments of glory, and invited to sit upon the heavenly throne. Here he has a crown placed upon his head, and is called "the lesser YHWH [Jehovah]" in the presence of his whole household.[11]

In the book of Abraham we have a classic account of a vision of the heavenly council. Indeed, in this instance what Abraham is shown is what Joseph Smith termed the Grand Council—the council held before the creation of the earth in which heavenly foreordinations were given. As Abraham was shown the vast host of spirits destined to come to the earth, he noted that there were many "noble and great ones." It was these that the Lord said he would make his rulers. To Abraham he said, "Thou art one of them; thou wast chosen before thou wast born." (Abraham 3:22–23.)

We have an apocryphal text, not found until long after Joseph Smith had translated the book of Abraham, which shows remarkable similarities to the vision recorded in Abraham 3. In this work, known as the Apocalypse of Abraham, the ancient prophet is shown all the children of earth at the time of the "Council." In this vision Abraham observes that the inhabitants of this premortal estate have been divided on the Lord's right hand and on his left; those on the right hand being destined to be the descendants of Abraham, or that lineage chosen to do the Lord's work, those on the left hand being destined for judgment and vengeance.[12]

The experience recorded in Abraham 3 was part of Abraham's preparation prior to his going into Egypt, where he was to "declare all these words" (Abraham 3:15). Recounting the experience, he said: "I, Abraham, talked with the Lord, face to face, as one man talketh with another; and he told me of the works which his hands had made; and he said unto me: My son, my son (and his hand was stretched out), behold I will show you all these. And he put his hand upon mine eyes, and I saw those things which his hands had made, which were many; and they multiplied before mine eyes, and I could not see the end thereof." (Abraham 3:11–12.)

Sent ones. The prophets of the Old Testament were called and chosen of the Lord—as we have seen illustrated in the calls of Moses, Isaiah, Jeremiah, and Ezekiel; they were his *sent ones* or, according to the Greek rendering of the word, his *apostles*. The Bible does not afford us a single instance in which a prophet is self-called or self-ordained. We are even without hint that those called of God anticipated or desired the call. In a number of instances they were openly reluctant. Their choosing was solely God's doing. Modern revelation affirms that such is the divine system, Joseph Smith stating it thus: "We believe that a man must be called of God, by prophecy, and by the laying on of hands by those who are in authority, to preach the Gospel and administer in the ordinances thereof" (Articles of Faith 1:5).

Divine commission. The very manner in which the gospel was restored in our dispensation is a perfect illustration that the ancient system required a call from God and the bestowal of authority by the laying on of hands by those holding it. Joseph Smith assumed no authority as a result of the First Vision or any other spiritual experience he had. Visions, dreams, revelations, as marvelous as they are, do not constitute authority or confer offices, keys, or power. In every instance the authority Joseph Smith professed was personally conferred upon him by the prophet or prophets holding that authority anciently. Each laid his hands upon Joseph's head and in blessing him identified the authority by which each acted and the specific authority that each was conferring upon him: John the Baptist in restoring the Aaronic Priesthood; Peter, James, and John in the restoration of the Melchizedek Priesthood; Moses in bestowing the keys by which Israel is to be gathered; an Elias from Abraham's dispensation granting the authority to perform eternal marriages; Elijah conveying the keys of sealing power; and so forth—each of the ancient prophets who restored keys making a personal appearance, each conferring the authority, rights, keys, honors, majesty, and glory he had enjoyed during his earthly ministry. Thus the ancients bestowed their authority as they had received it, this that the Lord's house might ever be a house of order. And in it all Joseph Smith was never alone. In compliance with the eternal law of witnesses another was always at his side when these authorities were conferred upon him. And so it must always be—within the kingdom of God there are no hidden offices or secret lines of authority (see D&C 42:11; 43:7).

The manner in which the ancients traced their authority back to God himself is restored to us for a pattern. Adam, Joseph Smith tells us, received the priesthood and its keys in the Creation.[13] Enoch, we know, was called of God (Moses 6:26–27), instructed in a heavenly vision (6:42), and ordained to the priesthood by Adam (D&C 107:48). As with Enoch, so with Noah, for we read: "The Lord ordained Noah after his own order, and commanded him that he should go forth and declare his Gospel unto the children of men, even as it was given unto Enoch" (Moses 8:19). Noah was ordained at the hands of Methuselah when only ten years old (D&C 107:52). Abraham received his priesthood from Melchizedek, who in turn traced his authority through Noah (D&C 84:14). Because Bible references to him are so few and terse, Melchizedek has remained an enigma to both students and scholars of the Bible alike. For Latter-day Saints this is not so—we know him as

> a man of faith, who wrought righteousness; and when a child he feared God, and stopped the mouths of lions, and quenched the violence of fire.
>
> And thus, having been approved of God, he was ordained an high priest after the order of the covenant which God made with Enoch,
>
> It being after the order of the Son of God, *which order came, not by man, nor the will of man;* neither by father nor mother; neither by beginning of days nor end of years; *but of God;*
>
> *And it was delivered unto men by the calling of his own voice, according to his own will, unto as many as believed on his name.*
>
> For God having sworn unto Enoch and unto his seed with an oath by himself; that every one being ordained after this order and calling should have power, by faith, to break mountains, to divide the seas, to dry up waters, to turn them out of their course;

To put at defiance the armies of nations, to divide the earth, to break every band, to stand in the presence of God; to do all things according to his will, according to his command, subdue principalities and powers; and this by the will of the Son of God which was from before the foundation of the world. . . .

And now, Melchizedek was a priest of this order. (JST, Genesis 14:26–33, italics added.)

Moses, who, as we have already noted, was called on Sinai and apparently endowed with power on the high mountain, was ordained to the priesthood by his father-in-law, Jethro (D&C 84:6). The last of the Old Testament prophets and the first of the New Testament was John the Baptist. He traced his priesthood in lineal descent from Aaron (D&C 84:27).

Admonition. Restored scripture detailing the commission given to the ancient prophets complies perfectly with the Old Testament examples, including the admonishing of the prophet after he has received the charge to go forth on the Lord's errand. "Go forth and do as I have commanded thee," the Lord said to Enoch, "and no man shall pierce thee. Open thy mouth, and it shall be filled, and I will give thee utterance, for all flesh is in my hands, and I will do as seemeth me good. . . . Behold my Spirit is upon you, wherefore all thy words will I justify; and the mountains shall flee before you, and the rivers shall turn from their course; and thou shalt abide in me, and I in you; therefore walk with me." (Moses 6:32–34.) To Abraham the Lord said, "I will lead thee by my hand, and I will take thee, to put upon thee my name, even the Priesthood of thy father,[14] and my power shall be over thee. As it was with Noah so shall it be with thee; but through thy ministry my name shall be known in the earth forever, for I am thy God" (Abraham 1:18–19). To Moses on the high mountain the Lord said, "Thou art after the similitude of mine Only Begotten," and Moses added "he also gave me commandments when he called unto me out of the burning bush, saying: Call upon God in the name of mine Only Begotten, and worship me." (Moses 1:16–17.)

New Testament: Calling of Prophets

One would expect among the Apostles and prophets of the New Testament a tracing of their authority to circumstances similar to those we have noted for prominent Old Testament prophets. In particular we would expect this of Christ, for it was he who gave the laws of discernment to the children of Israel. Let us first measure Christ against this standard, and then those who professed to represent him.

The high mountain experience. From the Joseph Smith Translation of the Bible we learn that Jesus, before he commenced his mortal ministry, was taken "in the Spirit" into an "exceeding high mountain," where he was shown marvelous visions (JST, Matthew 4:8). It will also be recalled that Christ took Peter, James, and John up "into an high mountain apart," where the Bible account tells us that he was transfigured before them (Matthew 17:1–9). A revelation given to Joseph Smith indicates that Peter, James, and John were also granted the privilege of seeing the earth as it would be at the time of its future transfiguration (D&C 63:21–22). We know that Paul was caught up to the third heaven (2 Corinthians 12:2–3). Joseph Smith explained that in this experience Paul obtained an understanding of "the three principal rounds of Jacob's ladder—the telestial, the terrestrial, and the celestial glories or kingdoms."[15] In the book of Revelation John refers to a similar experience. A door was opened in heaven, he said, and a voice spoke saying, "Come up hither, and I will shew thee things which must be hereafter. John then gives description of a "heavenly council" scene. (See Revelation 4:1–4.)

Sent ones. We have no more perfect illustration of one making profession to having been "sent" of God than Jesus of Nazareth. The book of John records over thirty instances in which Christ attests that he was sent of his Father. Such expressions are common to this testimony of himself: "My meat is to do the will of him that sent me, and to finish his work" (John 4:34). "I can of mine own self do nothing: as I hear, I judge: and my judgment is just; because I seek not mine own will, but the will of the Father which hath sent me" (John 5:30). "I came down from heaven, not to do mine own will, but the will of him that sent me" (John 6:38). "My doctrine is not mine, but his that sent me" (John 7:16). "I am not come of myself, but he that sent me is true, whom ye know not" (John 7:28). "Jesus cried and said, He that believeth on me, believeth not on me, but on him that sent me" (John 12:44).

To his Apostles (i.e., literally the "sent ones"), Christ said, "As my Father hath sent me, even so send I you" (John 20:21). "We must work the works of him who sent me, while it is day; night comes, when no one can work" (RSV, John 9:4). "Verily, verily, I say unto you, He that receiveth whomsoever I send receiveth me; and he that receiveth me receiveth him that sent me" (John 13:20). While the Gospels and Acts focus on the Twelve, the Epistles introduce Paul as an Apostle. "I am ordained a preacher," Paul declared, "and an apostle, (I speak the truth in Christ, and lie not;) a teacher of the Gentiles in faith and verity" (1 Timothy 2:7). Paul testified of Christ as the "Apostle and High Priest of our profession" (Hebrews 3:1). Indeed, in the broad and general sense, all within the pages of the New Testament who were properly commissioned to represent the Lord were spoken of as Apostles. One authority notes that "it is quite likely that our modern term 'missionary' is very close in meaning to the general use of 'apostle' in NT times."[16] An Apostle was understood to be an envoy, one sent on a mission to speak for the one sending him. All that the envoy did was to be done in the name and by the authority of the sender. He professed no authority or doctrine in his own name.

Divine commission. If we mark Christ's baptism at the hands of John the Baptist as the commencement of his ministry we would also mark it as the proper moment for him to identify the authority by which he would act. How perfect the story—as he comes up out of the waters of baptism the heavens are opened to him, and the Father introduces his

Son to the world, saying: "This is my beloved Son, in whom I am well pleased" (Matthew 3:17). There has been a similar pattern in at least two other dispensations. When Christ commenced his ministry among the Nephites, the Father introduced him, saying: "Behold my Beloved Son, in whom I am well pleased, in whom I have glorified my name—hear ye him" (3 Nephi 11:7). Again, in our own dispensation when the Father and Son appeared to Joseph Smith in the First Vision the Father introduced the Son by saying: *"This is My Beloved Son. Hear Him!"* (Joseph Smith—History 1:17).

Christ's parting act, according to the New Testament record, was a renewal of the commission given to the Apostles. "Go ye therefore, and teach all nations, baptizing them in the name of the Father, and of the Son, and of the Holy Ghost: teaching them to observe all things whatsoever I have commanded you: and, lo, I am with you alway, even unto the end of the world" (Matthew 28:19–20). The statement is perfect. The breadth of their commission is stated: "all nations"; their doctrine is delimited: "whatsoever I have commanded you"; their authority is declared: all that they did was to be done in the name of Jesus Christ; the ordinances of baptism or spiritual birth are announced with the reminder that in the performance of those ordinances they stood in the stead of the Father, the Son, and the Holy Ghost.

Admonition. There was nothing subtle in Christ's description of the reception the world would give those who came in his name. To the Twelve he said: "They shall deliver you up to be afflicted, and shall kill you, and ye shall be hated of all nations, for my name's sake" (Joseph Smith—Matthew 1:7). Earlier he had warned the disciples of the danger of being well thought of by the world. "Woe unto you, when all men shall speak well of you! for so did their fathers to the false prophets" (Luke 6:26). Having charged Peter to be true and faithful in teaching the gospel, Christ assured him of death by crucifixion (John 21:18–19). The principle was a simple one, and Christ had offered the explanation. "If the world hate you, ye know that it hated me before it hated you. If ye were of the world, the world would love his own: but because ye are not of the world, but I have chosen you out of the world, therefore the world hateth you." (John 15:18–19.)

Joseph Smith as Measured by the Bible Standard

In our day, Jew, Muslim, Catholic, and Protestant, each of whom profess to be the children of the book, have in turn announced the canon of scripture complete, the heavens sealed, and the last of the prophets come and gone. Though each normally whistles its own tune, theirs is a harmonious medley on the matter of living prophets—there can be none such!

How perfect the contrast! Joseph Smith also read the Holy Book and, reading it, believed: where it said "ask, and ye shall receive," Joseph asked; where it said "seek, and ye shall find," Joseph sought; where it said "knock, and it shall be opened unto you," Joseph knocked. He maintained this inquiring approach, and because of the responses he received Joseph Smith professed to be as much a prophet as was Moses, Isaiah, Jeremiah, or Ezekiel, and as much an Apostle as was Peter, James, and John. Thus he should be tested by the same standard. Let us then measure him as we would measure Moses, or Peter, or even Christ himself. Surely the requirement for being a prophet can be no less in our day than in times past. If the standard be good for one, it must be good for all. Jeremiah placed no statute of limitations on the test he gave for true prophets, nor do any of our Bible texts. We turn, then, to an evaluation of the divine commission claimed by Joseph Smith.

The high mountain or "heavenly council" experience. Joseph Smith in concert with Sidney Rigdon testified: "We beheld the glory of the Son, on the right hand of the Father, and received of his fulness; and saw the holy angels, and them who are sanctified before his throne, worshiping God, and the Lamb, who worship him forever and ever" (D&C 76:20–21). Such was the setting in which the glorious vision of the degrees of glory unfolded.

Describing another such experience Joseph said, "I beheld the celestial kingdom of God, and the glory thereof, whether in the body or out I cannot tell. I saw the transcendent beauty of the gate through which the heirs of that kingdom will enter, which was like unto circling flames of fire; also the blazing throne of God, whereon was seated the Father and the Son. I saw the beautiful streets of that kingdom, which had the appearance of being paved with gold." (D&C 137:1–4.) Then came the revelation of the marvelous truths that announced the conditions upon which those in the spirit world could accept the gospel unto salvation.

Yet the vision of angelic hosts and the celestial throne, even when attended by the revelation of heaven's most sacred mysteries, does not constitute a commission to act as God's envoy. Joseph claims revelation from the courts of heaven, but what of a divine commission? In response, we have already noted Joseph's teaching that "every man who has a calling to minister to the inhabitants of the world was ordained to that very purpose in the Grand Council of heaven before this world was," to which he added, "I suppose I was ordained to this very office in that Grand Council."[17] Though we are well within the bounds of biblical and historical evidence to suppose that all prophets were called and ordained in heavenly councils before birth, we are presently considering the earthly or mortal renewal of that call.[18] Be it remembered that Joseph Smith's profession to having obtained authority was confined to two settings—the wilderness and the temple. The Aaronic and Melchizedek Priesthoods, of necessity coming before the organization of the Church, were restored in the wilderness of the New York/Pennsylvania border, while all keys or authority coming subsequent to the erection of the Kirtland Temple were restored in that building. Clearly Moses, Elias, and Elijah could confer their authority in the earthly temple as readily as they could in its natural counterparts, of which it may be considered symbolic—the high mountain, the grove, or the wilderness. Describing the purpose of the Nauvoo Temple, the Lord said: "Let this house be built unto my name, that I may reveal mine ordinances therein unto my people; for I deign to reveal unto my church things which have been kept hid from before the foundation of the world, things that pertain to the dispensation of the fulness of times. And I will show unto my servant Joseph all things pertaining to this house, and the priesthood thereof, and the place whereon it shall be built." (D&C 124:40–42.)

Sent one. With the restoration of the priesthood and the organization of the Church came the charge—not to Joseph or the Twelve only, but to all to whom the priesthood would be given—to go forth and declare the restored gospel. "And now this calling and commandment give I unto you concerning all men—that as many as shall come before my servants Sidney Rigdon and Joseph Smith, Jun., embracing this calling and commandment, shall be ordained and sent forth to preach the everlasting gospel among the nations—crying repentance, saying: Save yourselves from this untoward generation, and come forth out of the fire, hating even the garments spotted with the flesh. And this commandment shall be given unto the elders of my church, that every man which will embrace it with singleness of heart may be ordained and sent forth, even as I have spoken." (D&C 36:4–7.)

Divine commission. As it was anciently, so it is today. "We believe that a man must be called of God, by prophecy, and by the laying on of hands by those who are in authority, to preach the Gospel and administer in the ordinances thereof" (Articles of Faith 1:5). Ours is a restored gospel. We profess no new principles—their faith is our faith; their doctrines are our doctrines, their priesthood our priesthood, their system of Church government our system of Church government. All that we have, we have received at their hands. Who else among the world's religious leaders professes to have received the authority to baptize from the Baptist himself? the authority of the higher or Melchizedek Priesthood from Peter, James, and John? the authority to gather Israel directly from Moses? the sealing power directly from Elijah? and so on? There is no uncertainty or ambiguity in the authority Joseph Smith held, or in its source.

Admonition. As the Lord promised Abraham that he would make his name great among all nations, so he promised Joseph Smith. Abraham was told that it would be his descendants that would be called upon to bear the ministry and priesthood, carrying the blessings of the gospel and salvation to all who would receive it (see Abraham 2:9, 11). Joseph Smith, being the prophet through whom the ancient covenants and the gospel were restored, was told that his name would be "had for good and evil among all nations, kindreds, and tongues, or that it should be both good and evil spoken of among all people" (Joseph Smith—History 1:33). Indeed, he was promised that the ends of the earth would inquire after his name, and that fools would have him in derision, and that all hell would rage against him, yet "the pure in heart, and the wise, and the noble, and the virtuous," would "seek counsel, and authority, and blessings" constantly from under his hand (D&C 122:1–2).

Since the Days of Joseph Smith

Two questions now demand answering: First, what of the successors of the Prophet Joseph Smith? Have they too stood in the heavenly council to receive message, mission, and admonition from the Lord? Second, what of the rest of us? Surely we do not have one doctrine for prophets and another for those who sustain and follow them. Are not the prophets but patterns of what ought to be true of all in the household of faith? If prophets are to be called in a particular manner, should not those who are to be in the image and likeness of the prophets be called in the same manner?

We will respond to the second question first. The answer is simply, yes. What is true of prophets ought to be true of all who have embraced the same faith and made the same covenants with their God. "What I say unto one I say unto all," the Lord has assured (D&C 93:49). What then of those called to the prophetic office? Must they have had a "heavenly council" or equivalent experience? If so, what evidence do we have of it?

The reader has probably already sensed that the experience of the prophets on the high mountain or in the heavenly council is for all intents and purposes the very experience enjoyed by all who ascend to the "hill of the Lord" (i.e., temple) to be "endowed with power from on high" (see D&C 38:32, 38; 39:15; 43:16; 95:8-9; 109:12-13, 22, 26). The endowment may well be the earthly renewal of covenants and promises once made in heavenly councils. Paul's epistle to the Ephesians seems to sustain such an idea. The faithful Saints, Paul wrote, were blessed "with all spiritual blessings in heavenly places in Christ: according as he hath chosen us in him before the foundation of the world, that we should be holy and without blame before him in love" (Ephesians 1:3-4).

Consistent with Joseph Smith's statement on premortal foreordination as quoted earlier in this chapter, President Joseph F. Smith's vision of the redemption of the dead specifically cites Joseph and Hyrum Smith, Brigham Young, John Taylor, and Wilford Woodruff as examples of men called and ordained in the councils of heaven before they were born into mortality. The revelation then expands the principle to embrace "other choice spirits who were reserved to come forth in the fulness of times to take part in laying the foundations of the great latter-day work" (D&C 138:53). Thus the prophets, with whose names and works we are familiar, serve as the example or illustration of the principle, yet the principle is no more exclusive to them than is baptism or any other gospel ordinance.

As to having been "sent" and "commissioned," let it suffice to say that all who will embrace the priesthood restored by Peter, James, and John to Joseph Smith and Oliver Cowdery "shall be ordained and sent forth to preach the everlasting gospel among the nations" (D&C 37:5). To such Christ has said, "You are mine apostles" (D&C 84:63). As to admonition, Wilford Woodruff addressed the quorum of the priesthood thus: "Let the Twelve Apostles, and the Seventy Apostles, and High Priest Apostles and all other Apostles rise up and keep pace with the work of the Lord God, for we have no time to sleep. What is a man's life good for, or his words or work good for when he stands in the way of men's salvation, exaltation, and glory?"[19]

Conclusions

1. There are elements common to the call of all prophets in all ages—Old Testament times, New Testament times, and today. Any professing to represent the Lord in our day must comply with the standard common to both Testaments of the Bible. As we have seen, there can be no profession to the prophetic office without revelation. God must call—the mission and commission must be his. Elements common to that experience among prophets have been the opening of the heavens, the temple or high mountain experience, the formal commission or sending forth, the giving of the messages they are to declare, and appropriate warnings or admonition.

2. It is also evident that the prophetic call cannot be confined to a single incident. The prophet's experience with the Lord is an ongoing one. Enoch's call, ordination, and ascension to the high mountain were three separate episodes. Moses was called and commissioned on Sinai, ordained by Jethro, and schooled on the high mount. Similarly, the meridian Twelve were converted, baptized, given the priesthood, called to the apostleship, and finally given the keys of the kingdom, all in an orderly fashion during the ministry of the Master. Christ also promised that they would be "endued with power from on high" after his ascension (see Luke 24:49; D&C 95:8–9).

3. Scripturally, Christ is the ultimate example of the nature and call of a prophet. We are repeatedly told of his foreordination, he being the "Lamb slain from the foundation of the world" (Revelation 13:8). He was administered to by angels (Mark 1:13), was "called of God an high priest after the order of Melchisedec" (Hebrews 5:10), and was caught up to the high mountain (JST, Matthew 4:8). He was the chief Apostle or "Sent One" (Hebrews 3:1). All that he did,

he did by the spirit of revelation. He was the mirror reflection of the mind and will of his Father (John 14:9).

4. Significantly, Joseph Smith's claim to authority perfectly combines the elements common to the call of his ancient counterparts. He claimed to have been called and ordained in the Grand Council of heaven, to have received his mission and commission directly from God, to have priesthood authority that traces to the divine throne, to preach nothing save that which was revealed to him, and to have been tutored and blessed at the hands of ancient prophets. Arguments against Joseph Smith do not center in his failure to claim such experiences, but rather in the fact that he claimed them. Those who have chosen to reject his claim do so on strength of the same arguments used by those who reject the ancient prophets.

5. As the nature of the prophetic call is the same in all ages, so is its purpose. The prophet's role is to bring men to God and God to men. Like the Savior, who was the personification of what all prophets strive to be, the prophet does not merely point the way to the divine presence but rather leads the way. The prophet and his followers tread the same path. There is not a high road for the prophet and a low road for his followers. All must climb Mount Zion, and in so doing all are entitled to the same endowment of divine power. Moses sought to sanctify all the nation Israel—men, women, and children—and so it must be in our day: all who wish to may obtain the fulness of gospel blessings by complying with the fulness of the gospel law.

Notes

1. Vine, *An Expository Dictionary of New Testament Words*, p. 63; Kittel and Friedrich, *Theological Dictionary of the New Testament*, pp. 67–68.

2. *Teachings*, p. 365.

3. *Teachings*, p. 181.

4. McConkie and Millet, *Doctrinal Commentary on the Book of Mormon*, 1:22–24.

5. Moses, like all prophets, was "sent" of God (Exodus 3:10). The word *sent* as rendered in the New Testament is *apostle*, an Apostle being "one sent forth." The Lord said, "I will send thee unto Pharaoh" (Exodus 3:10), and gave a token that they might know that "I have sent thee" (verse 12). In Egypt, Moses was to tell the Israelites that "the God of your fathers hath sent me," (verse 13), and when asked the name of his God he was to reply, "I AM hath sent me unto you" (verse 14).

6. The text reads "And *again*, the presence of the Lord appeared unto him" (JST, Exodus 3:2, italics added), the intimation being that this was not the first time that Moses had stood in the divine presence.

7. *Teachings*, p. 157.

8. *Teachings*, p. 158.

9. Schultz, "Angelic Opposition to the Ascension of Moses and the Revelation of the Law," p. 294.

10. Charlesworth, *The Old Testament Pseudepigrapha*, 1:139; 2 Enoch 22:8–9.

11. Charlesworth, *The Old Testament Pseudepigrapha*, 1:265; 3 Enoch 12:2–5.

12. Found in "The Book of the Revelation of Abraham," p. 715. For a recent translation, see R. Rubinkiewica, trans., "Apocalypse of Abraham," in Charlesworth, *The Old Testament Pseudepigrapha*, 1:681–705, especially p. 700.

13. *Teachings*, p. 157.

14. This is not a reference to Terah, Abraham's father, who was an idol worshipper, but rather to Abraham's righteous fathers through Noah (Abraham 1:1–3; 26).

15. *Teachings*, pp. 304–5.

16. Richards, *Expository Dictionary of Bible Words*, p. 60.

17. *Teachings*, p. 365.

18. Joseph Fielding McConkie, "Premortal Existence, Foreordinations, and Heavenly Councils," pp. 173–98.

19. *Journal of Discourses*, 4:147.

3

Prophets Foreknown

> *A choice seer will I raise up out of the fruit of thy loins, and he shall be esteemed highly among the fruit of thy loins. . . . And his name shall be called Joseph, and it shall be after the name of his father.*
> —JST, Genesis 50:27, 33
>
> *Behold, I will send my messenger, and he shall prepare the way before me.*
> —Malachi 3:1

Scriptural and historical evidence suggests that at the time of Christ many in the nation of Israel were anticipating the restoration of the gospel that has taken place in our dispensation through the Prophet Joseph Smith. This anticipation embraced the return of prophets who had once ministered among them, and the raising up of prophets from among their own number.

"Until a Trustworthy Prophet Should Arise"

First Maccabees, our primary source for Jewish history in the second century B.C., affirms an apostasy among the Jews and expresses the hope that the day will come when Israel will once again be blessed with the presence of prophets. It describes this era as one of "great distress in Israel, such as had not been *since the time that prophets ceased to appear among them*" (1 Maccabees 9:27, italics added).

After the death of Alexander the Great his empire was shared out among his friends and generals. Ptolemy, who received Egypt, soon secured Syria by conquest, but lost it to Seleucus after about twenty years. Palestine (among other conquests) was later added to the Seleucid empire. Attempts were then made to hellenize the Jews. The Book of Maccabees describes it thus: "In those days, lawless men came forth from Israel, and misled many, saying, 'Let us go and make a covenant with the Gentiles round about us, for since we separated from them many evils have come upon us.' This proposal pleased them, and some of the people eagerly went to the king. He authorized them to observe the ordinances of the Gentiles. So they built a gymnasium in Jerusalem, according to Gentile custom, and removed the marks of circumcision, and abandoned the holy covenant. They joined with the Gentiles and sold themselves to do evil." (1 Maccabees 1:11–15.)

Stephen E. Robinson writes:

> Finally, in 167 B.C., apparently with the full support of the reigning high priest, the Greek king of Syria-Palestine, Antiochus IV Epiphanes, outlawed the practice of circumcision and made it illegal to possess the Jewish scriptures. The temple at Jerusalem was converted to allow the worship of Zeus, and pigs were offered upon the altar in sacrifice to the pagan god. Greek soldiers were sent to the towns and villages of Judea to enforce the ban on traditional Judaism and to encourage the people to offer sacrifice to Zeus. The Greek king was extremely anxious that his Jewish subjects finally comply with hellenistic religious ideas and the hellenistic spirit of compromise.[1]

Such events precipitated a successful revolt by those zealous for the law and covenants of Israel, under the leadership of a family that came to be known as the Maccabees. Having recaptured their temple, "they cleansed the sanctuary and removed the defiled stones to an unclean place. They deliberated what to do about the altar of burnt offering, which had been profaned. And they thought it best to tear it down, lest it bring reproach upon them, for the Gentiles had defiled it. So they tore down the altar, and stored the stones in a convenient place on the temple hill *until there should come a prophet to tell what to do with them.*" (1 Maccabees 4:42–46, italics added.) One of the Maccabean brothers, Simon, was thereafter chosen as "the leader and high priest for ever, *until a trustworthy prophet should arise*" (1 Maccabees 14:41, italics added).

Ancient Prophets to Return

The preaching of John the Baptist in the wilderness of Judea caused no small stir among Jewish religious leaders. A delegation of "priests and Levites"[2] was quickly dispatched from the temple to ascertain who he was and by what authority he preached. The scriptural account of that interview, howbeit brief, is marvelously informative. At best it required a difficult day's journey simply to ask, "Who art thou?" Obviously they already knew who John was in a contemporary sense. The question suggests an anticipation that this wilderness prophet might claim to come in fulfillment of prophecy.

The first and most important question was, "Are you the promised Messiah?" The answer was immediate and direct: "I am not the Christ." "Are you Elijah?" came the second question. Again, the answer was in the negative. "Art thou that prophet?" was the third question, and for a third time John said no. (John 1:19–21.) Traditional commentary suggests that the third question was a restatement of the first. This is justified by the fact that Moses referred to Christ as a prophet (see Deuteronomy 18:18). If we are to accept that reasoning, the conversation was essentially this:

"Are you the Christ?"
"No!"
"Are you Elijah?"
"No."
"Are you the Christ?"
"No."

We are left to ask whether the temple delegation had such a short attention span that it was necessary for them to ask the same question twice, or whether each question referred to a separate part of the restoration they anticipated? Let us consider the second possibility and then return to complete the reading of the present text.

Be it remembered that near the conclusion of his ministry Christ, in the form of a testimony and missionary report meeting, asked the Apostles, "Whom do men say that I the Son of man am?" Surprisingly, a variety of responses was forthcoming: "Some say that thou art John the Baptist: some, Elias; and others, Jeremias, or one of the prophets" (Matthew 16:13–14).

Let us consider the implications of this informal opinion poll. Apparently many in the nation of Israel thought that Christ was really John the Baptist. The strange thing here is that John was dead and buried, and everyone knew it. The traditional response to this dilemma is to note that Herod Antipas, who put John to death, was haunted by the possibility that he had risen again (Matthew 14:2). Yet it was not Herod to whom the Apostles had been talking; it was the people, and the people had no need to fear John's ghost. Let us leave the matter unanswered for the moment and continue through the list.

Others held that Jesus of Nazareth was really Elijah. Such a notion was rooted in the prophecy of Malachi that Elijah, who was taken to heaven without tasting death, would return as an Elias to prepare the way for the coming of the Lord (Malachi 4:5–6). This is, of course, the reason why the temple delegation asked the Baptist whether he was Elijah.

Still another tradition among the Jews held that Jeremiah also would return to aid in the preparations for the coming of the Messiah. Before Israel was taken into the Babylonian captivity, the tradition said, Jeremiah took the ark and other sacred furniture from the temple and hid it in a cave on Mount Pisgah. He then sealed the cave and prophesied, "The place shall be unknown until God gathers his people together again and shows his mercy" (2 Maccabees 2:1–8). Since he had sealed the cave, it was assumed that he must break the seal and be the one to return the sacred items to the temple.

It was anticipated that other prophets also would return to be a part of events of such magnitude. The Apostles told the Savior that some of the people believed "one of the old prophets is risen again" (Luke 9:19). As to prophets who would come, tradition held that when Elijah returned, Moses would accompany him.[3] Edersheim adds Isaiah's name to the quorum of prophets who were expected to come back,[4] and it can certainly be reasoned from our present text that John the Baptist was numbered among this group. Given that it was prophesied that John would come to prepare the way for the Christ to come suddenly to his temple (Malachi 3:1), and that he would prepare the way for Christ's ultimate triumph (Isaiah 40:3–5; JST, Luke 3:4–11), neither of which were accomplished in their mortal ministries, it seems most natural that John's return would also be anticipated.

With Christ's dialogue with his Apostles as background let us now return to the question asked of the Baptist as to whether he was "that prophet." There can be no question that the Jews expected some of the ancient prophets to return as messengers of the long-hoped-for restoration. In this instance, however, a specific prophet is referred to, and because of the previous question we know it could not have been Elijah. Still another text allows us a feel for the expectations of the people. After Christ had preached a powerful sermon in the temple, many of the people said, "Of a truth this is the Prophet. Others said, This is the Christ." (John 7:40–41.)

Returning to the text in the Gospel of John, having asked the Baptist if he was the Christ, Elijah, or "that prophet," and having received a negative response to each question, the temple delegation returned to their first question, "Who art thou?" John's response was: "I am the voice of one crying in the wilderness, Make straight the way of the Lord, as said the prophet Esaias" (John 1:22–23).

Significantly, the interrogation of John continued. The question now became why he was baptizing if he was not the Christ, Elijah, or "that prophet". The implication of the question is far-reaching: First, it was obviously understood that when the Christ came he would come baptizing, that when Elijah came he would come baptizing, and when "that prophet" came he too would come baptizing. It was not a mere revival or reformation that the three were to bring, but rather a restoration—a movement requiring a new baptism.[5] Second, it appears that the anticipated restoration would involve the arrival of the three characters (Christ, Elijah, and the prophet), all of them coming on the scene at roughly the same time.

From textual restorations in the *Joseph Smith Translation* we learn that the Old Testament records once contained plain statements promising a restoration at the hands of prophets who long since had ministered among Israel. It will be remembered that Christ, near the conclusion of his ministry, took Peter, James, and John up onto what we know as the Mount of Transfiguration, where Elijah (rendered Elias in the New Testament text, because the Greek language does not allow the distinction between the two names) and Moses appeared to them. When they came down off the mountain, Peter asked the Savior why the scribes said that Elijah was to come at the beginning of his ministry rather than at its conclusion. In response Jesus said, "Elias truly shall first come, and restore all things, as the prophets have written. And again I say unto you that Elias has come already, concerning whom it is written, Behold, I will send my messenger, and he shall prepare the way before me; and they knew him not, and have done unto him whatsoever they listed. Likewise shall also the Son of Man suffer of them. But I say unto you, Who is Elias? Behold, this is Elias, whom I send to prepare the way before me. Then the disciples understood that he spake unto them of John the Baptist, and also of another who should come and restore all things, as it is written by the prophets." (JST, Matthew 17:10–14.)

Who then is "that prophet" whose coming was so closely associated with the coming of Christ, the return of Elijah, and the ordinance of baptism as John was practicing it? We are not without reason to suppose that it was the Prophet Joseph Smith. On Sunday, May 12, 1844, just a matter of weeks before his death, Joseph Smith preached a great discourse in defense of his role as a prophet. In the course of his remarks he picked up a German Bible and gave his audience a literal translation of Matthew 24:14. Having done so, he announced his translation to be more correct than its English counterpart and to be in harmony with the Latin, Greek, and Hebrew texts. In the King James Version the verse reads: "And this gospel of the kingdom shall be preached in all the world for a witness unto all nations; and then shall the end come." From the German, the Prophet rendered it thus: *"And it will preached be; the Gospel of the kingdom in the whole world, to a witness over all people, and then will the end come."* By way of commentary the Prophet explained that the Savior had taught that the gospel was to "be committed to a man, who should be a witness over the whole world, the keys of knowledge, power, and revelations, should be revealed to a witness who should hold the testimony to the world." Again he said, "All the testimony is, that the Lord in the last days would commit the keys of the Priesthood to a witness over all people."[6]

There is no question that in the context of his remarks Joseph Smith had reference to his own office and calling. Indeed, he said "I intend to lay a foundation that will revolutionize the whole world." By way of warning and further testimony, he said, "Woe! Woe! be to that man, or set of men, who lift up their hands against God and his Witness in these last days." The devil, the Prophet explained, always raises up false prophets to oppose the true prophets, and sets up his kingdom in opposition to the kingdom of God. It was in this discourse that Joseph Smith made his often-quoted statement about having been ordained to his office in the Grand Council of heaven?[7]

Only a brief synopsis of the Prophet's discourse was preserved for us—this by Thomas Bullock. A journal entry by George Laub, who was present in the meeting, sustains the Bullock notes and adds, "for Brother Joseph Smith was chosen for the last dispensation or Seventh Dispensation the time the Grand Council set in heaven to organize this world Joseph was chosen for the last & greatest Prophet to lay the foundation of God's work of the Seventh Dispensation therefore the Jews asked John the Baptist if he was Elias or Jesus or that great prophet that was to come."[8]

Prophecies of a Restoration

The Bible, both Old and New Testaments, is replete with prophecies about a latter-day restoration of the gospel and the kingdom of Israel. No prophet did more to detail this latter-day restitution of all things than did Isaiah. Indeed, it was Isaiah who, writing in the name of the Lord, commanded scattered Israel in a yet future day to listen to and accept the words of a prophet called from his mother's womb (i.e., foreordained) and known by name before his birth. This prophet, he said, would both gather Israel and be a light to the Gentiles. (Isaiah 49:1–11.)[9]

It was Joseph of Egypt who gave us the most explicit prophecy relative to this latter-day gathering and the prophet who would stand at its head. The Lord visited him and gave him the promise that out of the fruit of his loins he would raise up a righteous posterity and a choice seer who would bring Israel "out of darkness into light; out of hidden darkness, and out of captivity unto freedom." This choice seer, the ancient Joseph told us, was to do a labor not unlike his own and that of Moses. He was to restore the gospel in its purity and bring the Lord's people to salvation. Further, he was to bear the name Joseph after his ancient counterpart in Egypt and also after his own father. (JST, Genesis 50:24–33.)

No attempt will be made here to catalog the host of scriptural references prophesying of the latter-day restoration. However, two scriptural texts, both prophetic descriptions of the First Vision, ought be noted. The first comes from the pen of Jeremiah, who in the midst of a prophecy about the restoration of Israel in the last days at the hands of the tribe of Ephraim wrote: "Their prince will be one of their own, their ruler come from their own people. I will let him come freely into my presence and he can come close to me; who else, indeed, would risk his life by coming close to me?—it is Yahweh who speaks." (The Jerusalem Bible, Jeremiah 30:21.) The prophet is one of noble birthright, a prince of the tribe of Ephraim, who will approach the Lord and the Lord in turn will manifest himself to him. This is a matter of no small moment to an Old Testament writer, for it was well understood by that people that no unclean thing was to enter the presence of the Lord. Any unclean thing brought into his presence would be destroyed. As to a direct commentary on the passage, we turn to the words of an old Jewish writer who simply said: *"Certainly we could not blame any Jew who should see in these words a Messiah ben Joseph. This shall be in the latter days."*[10] (Later in this chapter we will return to a consideration of the Messiah ben Joseph tradition.)

Our second text is the JST rendering of Psalm 14, which also appears to be a prophetic description of the first vision. The first verse reads: "The fool hath said in his heart, there is no man that hath seen God. Because he showeth himself not unto us, therefore there is no God. Behold, they are corrupt; they have done abominable works, and none of them doeth good." The second verse has the Lord speaking from heaven to "his servant" asking if there are any who "understand God." The response is that many so profess. In the third verse the Lord says of those so professing that "they are all gone aside, they are together become filthy," and that "there are none of them that are doing good, no, not one." Continuing in the next verse the Lord says, "there is no knowledge in them." The Psalm concludes with the refrain: "Oh that Zion were established out of heaven, the salvation of Israel. O Lord, when wilt thou establish Zion? When the Lord bringeth back the captivity of this people, Jacob shall rejoice, Israel shall be glad."

The Samaritan Tradition of a Prophet of Restoration

A major tenet of Samaritan belief centers in the appearance at the end of time of *Taheb* (literally meaning "he who returns" or "he who causes to return"). This Ephraimite prophet (the Samaritans believe themselves to be of Ephraim) is to "restore everywhere the true law to its former validity and convert all peoples, especially the Jews, to the Samaritan religion."[11] A New Testament evidence of this tradition finds expression in the conversation between Christ and the Samaritan woman at Jacob's well. Christ had told the woman that she knew not what she worshipped. To which she responded, "I know that Messias cometh, which is called Christ: when he is come, he will tell us all things" (John 4:25). Her answer appears to be allusion to the belief in the coming of *Taheb* or "Restorer." "The *Taheb* is not a messiah in the Jewish sense of a deliverer or an anointed prince. Rather, he is like the prophet foretold in Deuteronomy 18:18, where God says: 'I will raise them up a Prophet from among their brethren, like unto thee, and will put my words in his mouth; and he shall speak unto them all that I shall command him.' He will appear to usher in a new dispensation, instruct the people in the law, restore the temple on Gerizim, reinstitute the sacrificial cult, and obtain the recognition of the heathen."[12]

The Essenes Anticipated the Coming of a Prophet

The Essenes, a Jewish sect not mentioned in the New Testament, dwelt in a secluded settlement on the north shore of the Dead Sea. It is from the pen of their scribes that we receive the Dead Sea Scrolls. They were religious refugees from Jerusalem, apparently in the days of the Maccabeans, whom they believed had usurped the office of high priest from the Zadokites in the year 152 B.C. One of the Zadokites, referred to as the Teacher of Righteousness, "may have openly fought this usurpation; and as a result, he and his followers either withdrew voluntarily or were forced to retreat to the shores of the Dead Sea, there to organize themselves into a community of 'the sons of light' to engage their opponents, 'the sons of darkness,' in a cosmic struggle. After their victory, they would reenter the destroyed Jerusalem to rebuild its temple according to the divine blueprint of the Temple Scroll and inaugurate a pure and correct ritual in accordance with its teachings."[13]

The Essenes viewed themselves as a covenant community—a community of Saints—anxiously awaiting the day of restoration. According to *The Manual of Discipline* the laws of the community were to be observed without modification, "until the coming of the Prophet and of both the priestly and the lay Messiah."[14] The restoration and their ultimate victory over darkness and evil centered in the coming of three key characters—a prophet, a priest (of the Levitical order), and a king or Messiah. Were we as Latter-day Saints to give credence to this prophecy it would be a rather natural interpretation to suggest that Joseph Smith was the expected prophet; John the Baptist, who restored the Aaronic Priesthood to Joseph Smith, the expected priest; and Jesus the Christ, who will rule during the millennial era, the lay Messiah or King.

The Essenes anticipated the coming of a great teacher of righteousness. Whether he was the same as the prophet or priests just mentioned is not clear. In any case, this ultimate "Teacher of Righteousness" was to be in the image of the original teacher of the community, who apparently had died a martyr. He was to be an expounder of the law and an interpreter of the scriptures, and to have seeric foresight. At least some authorities have concluded that his name was to be Asaph, the Hebrew form of Joseph. He was to be a forerunner to prepare a people to receive the Messiah.[15]

Jewish Traditions of a Messiah ben Joseph

Among the Jews of ancient days there was a tradition of a latter-day prophet who was to come on the scene at the end of time to restore Judah to Palestine and bring the lost tribes back to their lands of inheritance. Reference to this prophet, called Messiah ben Joseph, is found in the earliest of written sources. This anointed prophet was, as his name implies, to be a descendant of Joseph of Egypt. The tradition held that he would come on the scene before the coming of the Messiah ben David and attendant to the coming of Elijah. Along with his labors to gather Israel he was to restore true temple worship and then die a violent death at the hands of the enemies of Israel.

No part of the Messiah ben Joseph tradition was more important than the expectation of his death at the hands of his enemies. When Christian missionaries attempted to embarrass Jews by quoting Old Testament passages that spoke of Christ in his mortal ministry as a suffering servant, the Jews would respond that the passages were being misapplied: the Messiah that was to suffer the violent death was the Josephic Messiah, not the son of David for whom they waited. Their Messiah was to ascend above all things, not descend below them. The Christians countered the Jewish argument by saying that the Messiah ben Joseph was a tradition of late origin devised as a shield against the implications of the "suffering servant" passages. The discovery and translation of the Dead Sea Scrolls, with their reference to the coming of a prophet, the lay priest, and the lay Messiah, vindicated the Jewish position at least in that it pushed the Jewish expectation of dual Messiahs back to a considerable time before the birth of Christ.

The Jews themselves, however, cannot account for the origins of the tradition. References are made to the Messiah ben Joseph in both the Jewish and Babylonian Talmuds, but such works were not codified until the third century A.D., nor do they give any clues as to the origin of the tradition. In Talmudic sources the Messiah ben Joseph is mentioned only as an illustration to make another point. The story is told as if no explanation was needed because it was so well known by everyone. In later years a number of scriptural texts were suggested as its origin, including: the patriarchal blessing given to Joseph by Jacob (Genesis 49:22–26); the blessing given by Moses to the tribe of Joseph (Deuteronomy 33:13–17); Isaiah 53, which is a "suffering servant" passage that applies to Christ; and Ezekiel 37, which speaks of the sticks of Joseph and Judah that are one day to come together.

None of these passages, or the others cited, speaks of a chosen or anointed son of Joseph of Egypt who is to do a great work of restoration. Yet it cannot be lost upon the Latter-day Saint reader that with the coming of the Book of Mormon (the stick of Ephraim) and the work Joseph Smith did in his inspired translation of the Bible we have a prophecy that fits the Messiah ben Joseph tradition perfectly: a restoration of what should be the last chapter of Genesis, in which Joseph of Egypt tells of the Lord's visit to him and of the promises he then received relative to his posterity in the last days. The ancient Joseph was told that a latter-day descendant of his, one who would bear the name Joseph—which would also be the name of his father—would be instrumental in restoring the true gospel to the earth and in the gathering of Israel.[16] (JST, Genesis 50:24–38; 2 Nephi 3.) This prophecy was obviously once had among those in the Old World. Among other places, it was recorded on the brass plates, and thus was brought by Lehi and his family to the Americas.

The Ministry of Angels

The Jews at the time of Christ knew that previous gospel dispensations had centered in the appearance of angels who had been the source of their doctrines and authority. Through the revelations of the Restoration we know that Adam and others of his day had been taught the gospel by angels (Moses 5:58), that Enoch was taught in a like manner (Moses 7:27), and that three angels visited Abraham and Lot to instruct and bless them (Genesis 18:2; JST, Genesis 19:1).

Stephen in his dying testimony told those who stoned him that they had rejected the witness of the Holy Ghost as had their fathers before them. He challenged them with the question: "Which of the prophets have not your fathers persecuted?" Then he added, "They have slain them which shewed before of the coming of the Just One; of whom ye have been now the betrayers and murderers." As to the law of Moses, for which they professed such loyalty and reverence, Stephen said they had received it "by the disposition of angels, and have not kept it." (Acts 7:52–53.) Stephen's testimony, to which his Jewish antagonists did not object, was that the law of Moses—meaning its keys, powers, and authorities—had been granted to them at the hands of angels.

In responding to the influence of the Judaizers within the Church, Paul reminded the Galatian Saints that the law of Moses was "added" to the gospel law because of Israel's "transgressions." As to the Mosaic law, he said "it was ordained by angels in the hand of a mediator," again suggesting that Moses received it at the "hand of angels" (Galatians 3:19; JST, Galatians 3:19).

Angels to Herald the Return of Christ

It is not for Christ to return unknown and unseen. Indeed, "all the ends of the earth shall see the salvation [i.e., victory] of our God" (Isaiah 52:10; D&C 133:3). Enoch prophesied that the Lord would come "with ten thousands of his saints, to execute judgment upon all" (Jude 1:14–15).[17] John the Beloved by that same spirit of revelation described Christ's return to Mount Zion attended by a hundred and forty-four thousand, all of whom will have our Eternal Father's name written in their foreheads (Revelation 14:1).[18] Of that coming, Christ himself said: "I will reveal myself from heaven with power and great glory, with all the hosts thereof, and dwell in righteousness with men on earth a thousand years, and the wicked shall not stand" (D&C 29:11; see also JST, Matthew 24).

The matter of Christ's return is to be no secret. Heavenly messengers will herald the way before him. "He shall send his angels with a great sound of a trumpet, and they shall gather together his elect from the four winds, from one end of heaven to the other" (Matthew 24:31). John, who knew of the activities of these angels of the latter days, wrote testifying: "I saw another angel fly in the midst of heaven, having the everlasting gospel to preach unto them that dwell on the earth, and to every nation, and kindred, and tongue, and people, saying with a loud voice, Fear God, and give glory to him; for the hour of his judgment is come: and worship him that made heaven, and earth, and the sea, and the fountains of waters" (Revelation 14:6–7).

At a special conference for the elders of the Church in November 1831, the Lord announced through Joseph Smith that he had sent forth the angel spoken of by the Revelator. That angel, the Lord said, had appeared to some and would yet appear to others. Further, he had committed the everlasting gospel to men, and that gospel thus committed was now to be taken to all the inhabitants of the earth. "The servants of God shall go forth," the revelation stated, "saying with a loud voice: Fear God and give glory to him, for the hour of his judgment is come; and worship him that made heaven, and earth, and the sea, and the fountains of waters" (D&C 133:36–38).

It was never intended that a people be unprepared to receive their king. Surely this would be no less the case at the coming of the King of kings, and Lord of lords. If special messengers were sent to herald the advent of his mortal ministry, would we not expect the same and more to precede his second coming? Angels heralded his birth to humble shepherds in the fields of Judea, who in turn noised it abroad, becoming lifetime witnesses of his birth (Luke 2:8–17). "Angels are declaring it unto many at this time in our land," Alma declared of these ancient events, "and this is for the purpose of preparing the hearts of the children of men to receive his word at the time of his coming in his glory. . . . And it shall be made known unto just and holy men, by the mouth of angels, at the time of his coming, that the words of our fathers may be fulfilled, according to that which they have spoken concerning him, which was according to the spirit of prophecy which was in them." (Alma 13:24–26.)

Surely the announcement of Christ's mortal ministry to "just and holy men" constitutes the pattern of events to precede his return. As special witnesses, both angelic and mortal, prepared the way for him anciently, so such special witnesses will herald his second advent. Foremost among the meridian witnesses was John the Baptist, called even in

Prophets Foreknown

his birth "the prophet of the Highest," for he would "go before the face of the Lord to prepare his ways" (Luke 1:76). Nor was John's ministry confined to the events of mortality. He preceded Christ to the world of spirits and undoubtedly announced his coming among the faithful in that realm. It was also John's heaven-given destiny to return to earth in these the latter days to prepare the way of the Lord and make his paths straight. Only in John's return for this purpose do we find complete fulfillment of the prophecies relative to him.

Isaiah gave description of one who would preach in the wilderness and whose message would be the coming of the Lord. In that setting Isaiah said, "Every valley shall be exalted, and every mountain and hill shall be made low: and the crooked shall be made straight, and the rough places plain: and the glory of the Lord shall be revealed, and all flesh shall see it together: for the mouth of the Lord hath spoken it" (Isaiah 40:4–5). Our best commentary on these words of Isaiah is found in the Joseph Smith Translation of the third chapter of Luke. They read as follows:

> As it is written in the book of the prophet Esaias; and these are the words, saying, The voice of one crying in the wilderness, Prepare ye the way of the Lord, and make his paths straight.
>
> For behold, and lo, he shall come, as it is written in the book of the prophets, to take away the sins of the world, and to bring salvation unto the heathen nations, to gather together those who are lost, who are of the sheepfold of Israel;
>
> Yea, even the dispersed and afflicted; and also to prepare the way, and make possible the preaching of the gospel unto the Gentiles;
>
> And to be a light unto all who sit in darkness, unto the uttermost parts of the earth; to bring to pass the resurrection from the dead, and to ascend up on high, to dwell on the right hand of the Father,
>
> Until the fulness of time, and the law and the testimony shall be sealed, and the keys of the kingdom shall be delivered up again unto the Father;

> To administer justice unto all; to come down in judgment upon all, and to convince all the ungodly of their ungodly deeds, which they have committed; and all this in the day that he shall come;
>
> For it is a day of power; yea, every valley shall be filled, and every mountain and hill shall be brought low; the crooked shall be made straight, and the rough ways made smooth;
>
> And all flesh shall see the salvation of God. (JST, Luke 3:4–11.)

According to Isaiah's testimony, Christ was to come to gather Israel, prepare the way for the preaching of the gospel to the Gentiles, make possible the preaching of the gospel in the spirit world (referred to here as "the uttermost parts of the earth"), bring to pass the resurrection from the dead, and ascend to dwell on the right hand of the Father. Then, in the fulness of times, he was to come again, in this instance to administer justice to all, and to convince the ungodly of their ungodly deeds. This would be the day of his power, the day in which every valley would be filled, every mountain and hill brought low, the crooked made straight, and the rough made smooth. This would be the day in which all flesh should see the ultimate victory of Christ. Though Isaiah's words can be applied to the mortal ministry of Christ, they could also find a measure of fulfillment in John the Baptist as an Elias being involved in preparing the way for the second coming of Christ.

Malachi also spoke of a messenger who was to come to prepare the way before the Christ. As with the Isaiah prophecy, the New Testament applies this text to the Baptist and his role as forerunner of the mortal Christ (Matthew 11:10; Mark 1:2). To such an interpretation we can but say "Amen," yet we note that the prophecy reaches beyond such events. The context of the prophecy is that of the Lord suddenly coming to his temple and the wicked being unable to abide his presence. It is to be in a day of restoration when the sons of Levi, having been purified, will offer again an offering unto the Lord in righteousness. That this has reference to the Second Coming there can be no doubt. It was for this very purpose of restoring the lesser priesthood that John the Baptist appeared to Joseph Smith and Oliver Cowdery on May 15, 1829. Laying his hands upon their heads, he said: "Upon you my fellow servants, in the name of Messiah I confer the Priesthood of Aaron, which holds the keys of the ministering of angels, and of the gospel of repentance, and of baptism by immersion for the remission of sins; *and this shall never be taken again from the earth, until the sons of Levi do offer again an offering unto the Lord in righteousness*" (D&C 13:1–2, italics added). It is generally accepted in the Church that the messenger referred to by Malachi, who would prepare the way for Christ's second coming, was Joseph Smith, the great Prophet of the last dispensation. But that would in no way preclude John the Baptist's also having a role as an Elias for the Second Coming. Indeed, as shown above, it was John who restored the authority whereby the sons of Levi are to be purified (i.e., baptized) that they might receive the priesthood and perform acceptable sacrifices to the Lord.[19]

That the second coming of Christ also required a second coming of John to help prepare the way for him is further evidenced by the tradition among the meridian Jews that John would return. This is the only sensible explanation of the report given by the Apostles to Christ when he asked who men said that he was. They responded that some people said that he was John the Baptist, though they all knew that John had been beheaded.

Though the second coming of the Baptist as an Elias of the Second Coming may be a matter of conjecture, the coming of Elijah is not. That Elijah is to return prior to "the great and dreadful of the Lord" is the plain announcement of scripture (Malachi 4:5). Though the Christian world in general has supposed that this prophecy was fulfilled when Elijah appeared on the Mount of Transfiguration (Matthew 17:3–4), the time of that event hardly satisfies the description of a "great and dreadful day," nor does it comply with the context of Malachi's prophecy as the day in which the proud and the wicked are to be burned as stubble (Malachi 4:1).

The book of Revelation also announces the coming of prophets in the last days. An angel of God instructed John that he was to "prophesy *again* before many peoples, and nations, and tongues, and kings" (Revelation 10:11, italics added). Revelations given to Joseph Smith provide considerable understanding relative to John's commission. In April 1829 the Prophet learned that John had not tasted of death but instead had been translated. "I will make him as flaming fire," the Lord told Peter, "and a ministering angel; he shall minister for those who shall be heirs of salvation who dwell on the earth" (D&C 7:6). Three years later the Lord expanded Joseph's understanding in a revealed explanation of Revelation chapters 10 and 11.

> Q. What are we to understand by the little book which was eaten by John, as mentioned in the 10th chapter of Revelation?
> A. We are to understand that it was a mission, and an ordinance, for him to gather the tribes of Israel; behold, this is Elias, who, as it is written, must come and restore all things.
> Q. What is to be understood by the two witnesses, in the eleventh chapter of Revelation?
> A. They are two prophets that are to be raised up to the Jewish nation in the last days, at the time of the restoration, and to prophesy to the Jews after they are gathered and have built the city of Jerusalem in the land of their fathers. (D&C 77:14–15.)

Conclusions

1. Whenever the gospel has been bequeathed from heaven to men, it has come by revelation to prophets, with its keys and authorities coming at the hands of angels. This pattern was so well established in Old Testament times that the nation of Israel was anticipating such a dispensing of heavenly powers at the hands of ancient prophets when John the Baptist and Christ came on the scene to commence the meridian dispensation. Prophecies and traditions then exis-

tent among the Jews give us reason to suspect that at least in some measure they anticipated the very restoration that has taken place in our own dispensation.

2. If there is to be a restoration of the kingdom of Israel, as the united voice of the prophets proclaims, there must be a restoration of the prophetic office. Nothing less will satisfy the promises made and prophecies given. Nothing less will meet the needs of a covenant people gathered to honor their God. Governments and churches may arise claiming to be the fulfillment of the prophecies that the kingdom of Israel would be restored, but without prophets such claims are as an ocean without water or a banquet without food.

3. The latter-day "restitution of all things," which we know was known to and spoken of "by the mouth of all [the] holy prophets since the world began" (Acts 3:21), assumes an opening of the heavens and the calling of prophets. Without prophets there could be no restoration. The life of that kingdom whose restoration we are promised centers in and around the temple and the inspired leadership of prophets. To restore that kingdom without temples and prophets would be like a resurrection of the body without the spirit. It simply would be without life or purpose. A restoration of the kingdom of Israel without the religion of Israel could no more qualify as a restoration of the original kingdom than a painting of Christ could satisfy the prophecies of his return or a depiction of the temple could substitute for the house of the Lord.

Notes

1. Robinson, "The Setting of the Gospels," p. 15.
2. This combination is not found elsewhere in the New Testament. The probability is that they represented the Sanhedrin.
3. Ginzberg, *The Legends of the Jews*, 3:141; 6:167.
4. Edersheim, *The Life and Times of Jesus the Messiah*, 2:707 n. 2.
5. From modern revelation we know that baptism was commonly practiced among the Jews at that time as the following text illustrates: "Then said the Pharisees unto him, Why will ye not receive us with our baptism, seeing we keep the whole law? But

Jesus said unto them, Ye keep not the law. If ye had kept the law, ye would have received me, for I am he who gave the law. I receive not you with your baptism, because it profiteth you nothing. For when that which is new is come, the old is ready to be put away." (JST, Matthew 9:18–21.)

6. Ehat and Cook, *The Words of Joseph Smith*, p. 366; this discourse can also be found in *History of the Church*, 6:363–64, and *Teachings*, pp. 364–65.

7. Ehat and Cook, p. 367.

8. Ehat and Cook, p. 370.

9. For a detailed consideration of this prophecy, see McConkie and Millet, *Doctrinal Commentary on the Book of Mormon*, 1:157–58.

10. King, *The Yalkut on Zechariah*, p. 87, italics added.

11. Klausner, *The Messianic Idea in Israel*, p. 484.

12. Ricks, "No Prophet Is Accepted in His Own Country," p. 207–8.

13. Milgrom, "The Dead Sea Temple Scroll," pp. 63–64.

14. Gaster, *The Dead Sea Scriptures*, p. 63.

15. Bruce, *Second Thoughts on the Dead Sea Scrolls*, pp. 92–97.

16. For a more detailed account of the Messiah ben Joseph tradition with the sources from which it comes, see J. F. McConkie, *His Name Shall Be Joseph*.

17. This passage is found in 1 Enoch 1:9 and reads as follows: "And behold! He comes with ten thousand holy ones to execute judgement upon them, and to destroy the impious, and to contend with all flesh concerning everything which the sinners and the impious have done and wrought against him." (Sparks, *The Apocryphal Old Testament*, p. 185.) A variant translation of the verse reads thus: "Behold, he will arrive with ten million of the holy ones in order to execute judgment upon all. He will destroy the wicked ones and censure all flesh on account of everything that they have done, that which the sinners and the wicked ones committed against him." (See Charlesworth, *The Old Testament Pseudepigrapha*, 1:13–14.)

18. Through modern revelation we know that the hundred and forty-four thousand spoken of by John (Revelation 7:4) are high priests whose calling and election has been made sure (see D&C 77:11; *Teachings*, p. 321).

19. For further explanation as to the necessity of such sacrifices, see *Teachings*, pp. 172–73.

4

The Discerning of Prophets

> *Beware of false prophets, which come to you in sheep's clothing, but inwardly they are ravening wolves.*
> —Matthew 7:15
>
> *He that receiveth a prophet in the name of a prophet shall receive a prophet's reward.*
> —Matthew 10:41

"False prophets," stated Joseph Smith, "always arise to oppose the true prophets and they will prophesy so very near the truth that they will deceive almost the very chosen ones."[1] The principles of salvation are always opposed by the adversary. Whenever there is a dispensation of the gospel, the devil "always sets up his kingdom at the very same time in opposition to God."[2] Prophetically our dispensation had been described as one in which false Christs and false prophets would "show great signs and wonders, insomuch that, if possible, they shall deceive the very elect, who are the elect according to the covenant" (Joseph Smith—Matthew 24:23).

This warning against false Christs is primarily a warning against false notions and doctrines about Christ and that gospel we received from him. In like manner, the warning about false prophets is primarily a warning against false notions relative to the office and calling of prophets and the doctrines received from them. The necessity of discerning false Christs and prophets affirms the reality that not all systems of worship, even if sustained with sincerity, are acceptable to the Lord. Further, it assures that an association with the true Christ and his prophets is possible.

How Are We to Judge?

By what means are we to distinguish between true and false prophets? The justice of God demands that all accountable persons be capable of judging all professions to the prophetic office. Yet the matter is not so obvious that the undiscerning cannot be deceived. The scriptures sound their warning to the "very elect," and all of us know seemingly good and well-intentioned people who have been duped by spiritual frauds. What then is the sure standard by which we are to "try the spirits" (1 John 4:1)?

It should not go unnoticed that tests given in the Bible by which prophets are to be discerned have been used to reject true prophets more often than false ones. Christ was rejected by the use of such tests. He was condemned for blasphemy against the very law he gave Moses on Sinai. What is true of Christ has also been true of the greater part of the prophets who have come in his name. They too have been rejected in the name of loyalty to the Bible and by the misuse of tests it gives for the discerning of prophets. The lesson in all of this is simply that no test for the discerning of prophets is any better than the spirit and wisdom by which the test is applied. There are no truths to which someone cannot bring seemingly plausible and defensible objections. Further, just as the truths of salvation will never go unopposed, neither will those commissioned to convey them.

Significantly, tests used by Christian writers to prove Joseph Smith a false prophet and Mormonism a spiritual hoax produce similar results when applied to Christ and Christianity. One such writer, in a work titled *The New Cults*, lists ten characteristics of a cult as follows:

1. Strong leaders
2. The claim to additional scripture
3. Maintaining rigid standards for members
4. A membership consisting largely of converts
5. Active proselytizing
6. Having no professional clergy
7. Being in a "state of flux" (i.e., no fixed creed)

The Discerning of Prophets

  8. A belief in continual revelation
  9. The exclusive claim to possession of the truths of salvation
  10. Possession of a cultic vocabulary[3]

By such a standard Christ and the Church organized by him in the meridian of time stand convicted on all counts.

(1) Christ was a strong leader, as were Peter, Paul, and the other great characters of the New Testament Church.

(2) As to scripture, members of the meridian Church freely penned it, their words being preserved for us in the form of the New Testament.

(3) As to "rigid standards," we need but turn to the Sermon on the Mount, where Christ repetitiously said, "It hath been said by them of old time" we are to do this or that, "but I say unto you" such and such. Then he gave a higher standard than the Mosaic code, a code famed for its strictness.

(4) In its first generation all within the Church Christ organized were converts.

(5) Thereafter the Church continued to be a convert Church, with the obligation to take the message of the gospel to every nation, kindred, tongue, and people.

(6) The meridian Church had no professional clergy, and the teaching of the gospel for hire was specifically forbidden (Matthew 10:8; 1 Corinthians 9:18; 2 Corinthians 11:7).

(7) Because they had living prophets and the spirit of revelation, creedal statements were unknown in the meridian Church, as was the idea of a closed canon. In one instance missionaries were directed to go out without purse or scrip, in another they were commanded to take purse and scrip (Luke 10:4; 22:35–36). When the Twelve were called to their ministry they were specifically forbidden to teach Gentiles; later they were charged to labor among them (Matthew 10:1–6; Mark 16:14–20). Such is the "doctrinal flux" to which our critic appears to object.

(8) At the Last Supper Christ promised his disciples the companionship of the Holy Ghost, by which they would be guided into all truth and be shown that which was to come

(John 16:12–14). Indeed, the Holy Ghost is a revelator, and all who company with him receive revelation. To argue that revelation has ceased is to acknowledge that the Holy Ghost no longer finds you fit company.

(9) As to that narrowness that results in the claim to an exclusive possession of the path leading to salvation, we are reminded of the words of the Master: "I am the way, the truth, and the life: no man cometh unto the Father, but by me" (John 14:6); and "strait is the gate, and narrow is the way, which leadeth unto life, and few there be that find it" (Matthew 7:14).

(10) And finally, as to a cultic vocabulary, what better illustration than the New Testament Church, in which we find such expressions as "baptism," "church," "Christ," "resurrection," "Holy Spirit" or "Holy Ghost," none of which are found in the Old Testament?

Scriptural history is consistently at odds with popular perceptions of the nature and characteristics of prophets. Consider the matters of appearance and personality, eloquence, environs and background, family, scholastic training, and public acceptance.

Appearance and personality. Though the scriptures contain no description of Jesus of Nazareth, we do learn from a prophecy of Isaiah's that there would be nothing in his physical appearance that would draw people to him (Isaiah 53:2). The Septuagint rendering of this prophecy states that his form would be "ignoble, and inferior to that of the children of men" (Isaiah 53:3), while the New English Bible states that he would be without "grace to make us delight in him." Clearly, people were not to be attracted to Jesus' profession to Messiahship on the basis of physical appearance or what the world calls charisma. It is not intended that we confuse the message with the messenger.

John, who came wearing a rough garment of camel's hair with a leather belt, was hardly stylish even for his day; nor was his diet of locusts and wild honey particularly savory (Matthew 3:4). Be it also remembered that Samuel was scolded by the Lord for supposing that Eliab should be anointed Israel's king because his appearance and bearing impressed Samuel as being kingly. "Look not on his countenance, or on the height of his stature . . . ," The Lord instructed Samuel, "for the Lord seeth not as man seeth; for man looketh on the outward appearance, but the Lord looketh on the heart" (1 Samuel 16:7).

As to our more modern day, we need but read Wilford Woodruff's description of Brigham Young and Heber C. Kimball as they commenced their prophetic ministry in the British Isles. They were, Elder Woodruff writes, "without a second suit to their backs, for the mob in Missouri had taken all they had." Brigham's wardrobe "had not much of a ministerial appearance." His cap had been made out of "a pair of old pantaloons," while he found it necessary to wrap himself in a quilt, not owning an overcoat.[4] As humble as their situation was, it would have to be considered better than that of the youthful Joseph F. Smith and his missionary companion in Hawaii, who had all their belongings destroyed in a fire. Left with one suit between them, they took turns wearing it. One Elder would stay in bed while the other one labored, and then they would change places.[5]

Eloquence. Enoch was "slow of speech" (Moses 6:31), Moses required a spokesman (Exodus 4:14–15), and Jeremiah tried to beg out of his call, saying, "I cannot speak" (Jeremiah 1:6). Writing to the Corinthian Saints, the Apostle Paul said: "I was with you in weakness, and in fear, and in much trembling" (1 Corinthians 2:3–4). In his early years Joseph Smith was given a spokesman (D&C 100:9–11). The feelings common to those called of God to bear his message were articulately expressed by the inarticulate Heber C. Kimball when he was designated as the first missionary of our dispensation to cross the ocean and declare the gospel in a foreign land: "O, Lord, I am a man of stammering tongue, and altogether unfit for such a work; how can I go to preach in that land [England], which is so famed throughout Christendom for learning, knowledge and piety; the nursery of religion; and to a people whose intelligence is proverbial!"[6] Yet many years later, as he reflected on the marvelous success he and his fellow missionaries had enjoyed on that mission in declaring the message of the Restoration, Elder Kimball observed: "The Lord appointed me to that work because I was willing to be the simplest."[7] Simple and unrefined in the worldly sense, the messengers of the Lord are to trust in the spirit and power of their message to touch the hearts and change the lives of those to whom they are called to preach.

Background and environs. Moses fled into the desert after slaying an Egyptian taskmaster; Paul was responsible for the imprisonment and death of both men and women who had chosen to follow Christ; Alma and the sons of Mosiah led many into paths of rebellion and disobedience. Each was destined to become a valiant servant in the gospel cause.

Certainly there was nothing pretentious in Christ's background. He was born in a stable, was raised as a carpenter's apprentice, was unschooled in the learning of men, and he hailed from—of all places—Nazareth of Galilee. His were not impressive credentials.

Family. Terah, the father of Abraham, refused his son's message of repentance and in conspiracy with others of his family sought Abraham's life at the hand of the priest of Elkenah. Only divine intervention prevented Abraham from being offered as a sacrifice to the Egyptian and Chaldean gods (Abraham 1:15–17). Hosea was commanded of the Lord to take "a wife of whoredoms" (Hosea 1:2). During his mortal ministry Jesus' brothers rejected his claim to Messiahship (John 7:5).

Scholastic training. Of Christ it was said, "How knoweth this man letters, having never learned?" (John 7:15), meaning that he had not received the training and instruction expected of a rabbi. For his Apostles he chose humble fishermen from Galilee. As it is for the Lord to call his own agents, so it is for him to educate them in his work and his ways.

Public acceptance. The world loves and honors its own. Such acclaim is not accorded prophets. The world chooses to hear those who speak its own doctrines. John taught the principle thus: "They are of the world: therefore speak they of the world, and the world heareth them. We are of God: he that knoweth God heareth us; he that is not of God heareth not us. Hereby know we the spirit of truth, and the spirit of error." (1 John 4:5–6.)

The Profile of a Prophet

As we span the horizon of history we see that perhaps no group of men have been so diverse and yet shared so much in common as have the prophets of the Lord. Let us identify those characteristics that are common to prophets of all ages, characteristics by which true prophets may always be known.

First, prophets must be righteous men. No principle was better understood among Old Testament peoples than that no unclean thing could stand in the presence of God. Finding himself in the divine presence, Isaiah declared, "Woe is me! for I am undone [meaning, I am lost]; because I am a man of unclean lips, and I dwell in the midst of a people of unclean lips: for mine eyes have seen the King, the Lord of hosts." Whereupon a ritual of purification was performed in order that he not be destroyed. (Isaiah 6:5–6.) It will be remembered that Hagar manifested surprise that she had stood in the presence of an angel of the Lord and had not been destroyed (NEB, Genesis 16:12); and that after an angel of the Lord appeared to Manoah and his wife, Manoah said, "We shall surely die, because we have seen God," while his wife argued that the Lord was pleased with them, for he had accepted their sacrificial offering (Judges 13:22–23). All distinctions in the Mosaic code as to what was ritually clean or unclean shared the same purpose—to teach that purity was a necessary requisite to entering the divine presence.

Thus we find the Lord saying to the early elders of this dispensation:

> It is your privilege, and a promise I give unto you that have been ordained unto this ministry, that inasmuch as you strip yourselves from jealousies and fears, and humble yourselves before me, for ye are not suffi-

ciently humble, the veil shall be rent and you shall see me and know that I am—not with the carnal neither natural mind, but with the spiritual.

For no man has seen God at any time in the flesh, except quickened by the Spirit of God.

Neither can any natural man abide the presence of God, neither after the carnal mind.

Ye are not able to abide the presence of God now, neither the ministering of angels; wherefore, continue in patience until ye are perfected. (D&C 67:10–13.)

In a subsequent revelation the Lord told them that it was this state of sanctity that Moses sought to have Israel obtain so that they, as a nation, might see their God, but that they would not, and thus Moses and the Melchizedek Priesthood were taken from them (D&C 84:20–25).

In another expression of the same principle the Lord said "that the rights of the priesthood are inseparably connected with the powers of heaven, and that the powers of heaven cannot be controlled nor handled only upon the principles of righteousness" (D&C 121:36). Thus righteousness and the prophetic spirit are inseparable. True prophets must be worthy of both God's Spirit and his presence. Paul said it thus: "They which preach the gospel should live of the gospel" (1 Corinthians 9:14).

Second, the motives of true prophets will be pure. Prophets are called by the voice of God, not by their own will. Scriptural accounts indicate that their native disposition was often much averse to the calling that came to them. "Why is it that I have found favor in thy sight?" Enoch asked. "[I] am but a lad," he said, "and all the people hate me; for I am slow of speech; wherefore am I thy servant?" (Moses 6:31.) "Who am I, that I should go unto Pharaoh?" Moses asked of the Lord when he was called to lead the children of Israel from their Egyptian bondage (Exodus 3:11).

Never do we read of prophets calling themselves into that service. To the Twelve in his day Christ said: "Ye have not chosen me, but I have chosen you, and ordained you, that ye should go and bring forth fruit, and that your fruit should remain: that whatsoever ye shall ask of the Father in my name, he may give it you" (John 15:16). Such is the everlasting order; it is for God to choose his servants and it is for him to determine their message. Worldly honors and adulations are not associated with the prophetic office.

The Didache (i.e., the Teachings), an early Christian work, reflects the attitude of the meridian Church relative to the purity of purpose that was expected of those professing to be ministers of the Lord. "Every missioner who comes to you should be welcomed as the Lord, but he is not to stay more than a day, or two days if it is really necessary. If he stays for three days, he is no genuine missioner. And a missioner at his departure should accept nothing but as much provisions as will last him to his next night's lodging. If he asks for money, he is not a genuine missioner." Further, it was written that "if his deeds do not correspond with his words he is an impostor."[8] In short, those who represent the Lord do so for the Lord's purposes, not their own. The Lord has commanded that there "be no priestcrafts; for, behold, priestcrafts are that men preach and set themselves up for a light unto the world, that they may get gain and praise of the world; but they seek not the welfare of Zion" (2 Nephi 26:29).

Third, all true prophets will be revelators. As the prophet's call must trace itself to heaven, so must his message. The prophet's words are to reflect the mind of the Lord. Christ established the pattern: "My doctrine is not mine, but his that sent me. If any man will do his will, he shall know of the doctrine, whether it be of God, or whether I speak of myself. He that speaketh of himself seeketh his own glory: but he that seeketh his glory that sent him, the same is true, and no unrighteousness is in him." (John 7:16–18.)

Fourth, though the call to the prophetic office appears to have been permanent, prophets have not supposed themselves to be inspired at all times and on all matters. Joseph Smith taught that a prophet was a prophet only when acting as such.[9] It was never intended that prophets be excused from the vicissitudes of life or be placed above the possibility of mistake or error. "Condemn me not because of mine imperfection," wrote Moroni, "neither my father, because of his imperfection, neither them who have written before him; but rather give thanks unto God that he hath made manifest unto you our imperfections, that ye may learn to be more wise than we have been" (Mormon 9:31).

The scriptures do not teach a doctrine of prophetic infallibility. When David told Nathan that he had decided to build a temple, Nathan said, "Go, do all that is in thine heart; for the Lord is with thee." That night Nathan learned that the Lord did not want David to build the temple, for that privilege was to be reserved for David's son. Nathan then reversed himself on the matter. (2 Samuel 7:3–16). Similarly, God ordered Samuel to go to Bethlehem and anoint one of Jesse's sons to replace Saul as king. Samuel's initial impression was to anoint Jesse's oldest son, Eliab. This, however, did not represent the will of the Lord, who redirected the mind of the prophet to choose Jesse's youngest son, David. (1 Samuel 16.) Again, a truly prophetic statement may be changed by its author—the Lord. Isaiah told Hezekiah, in the name of the Lord, that he was to die. But Hezekiah prevailed upon the Lord for an extension of his life, and Isaiah was then directed to return and tell him he would live another fifteen years. (See Isaiah 38:1–5.)

Prophets are subject to the weaknesses and temptations common to all men (see Acts 14:14–15; James 5:17). "Although a man may have many revelations," the Lord said, "and have power to do many mighty works, yet if he boasts in his own strength, and sets at naught the counsels of God, and follows after the dictates of his own will and carnal desires, he must fall and incur the vengeance of a just God upon him" (D&C 3:4).

Fifth, prophets are normally found in opposition to the established orthodoxy of the day. Often it is the role of prophets to oppose the most cherished of institutions against seemingly impossible odds. It was for Abraham, the fugitive of Ur, to bear the name of the Lord in a strange land among a strange people; it was for the inadequate tongue of Moses the shepherd of Sinai to withstand the might of Egypt; it was for the unschooled Galilean to challenge the learned rabbis and the fortress of traditions they had built around the law of Moses; it was for the diminutive Paul to contend with the learning and wisdom of the Greeks; and it was for the youthful Joseph Smith to announce that the creeds of Christendom were an abomination in the sight of God and that their professors were all corrupt. Indeed, it is the heavenly pattern for the Lord to choose the weak things of the earth to oppose the mighty and strong ones.

Sixth, though true prophets are always at odds with the philosophies of men, their commission is not to destroy but to build. Christ came to fulfill the law of Moses, not to destroy it. In fulfilling the law he ratified the sanctity of that which he had revealed to Moses. Yet his actions were construed as a threat to it. The Book of Mormon is a modern parallel. The Lord specifically stated that its purpose is to sustain and defend the Bible (D&C 20:11; 2 Nephi 3:11). Yet it is constantly argued by many who profess a reverence for the Bible that the Book of Mormon was written to destroy it. The Book of Mormon no more seeks to destroy the Bible than Christ did the law of Moses. Testifying of the purpose of the Book of Mormon the Lord said: "Behold, I do not bring it to destroy that which they have received, but to build it up" (D&C 10:52, 62). So it is with all the truths of heaven—their purpose is to build, not to destroy. It is characteristic of good doctrine that it lifts rather than suppresses, brings joy and peace to the righteous rather than sorrow or discomfort. Good doctrine encourages rather than discourages; it is always the companion of light, never the companion of darkness.

The true prophet builds a more perfect place to house our faith and leaves it to us to abandon our old abode. The false prophet sets the flame of his wrath to our house, promising us nothing but liberation from what we once enjoyed. The one builds, the other destroys.

Seventh, it is the law of heaven that no testimony as to new revelation is to stand alone, but rather that the truth in all such mat-

ters is to be established in the mouths of two or more witnesses. There are no exceptions: the message of all who would claim themselves prophets must comply with his heaven-given standard. It is for this very reason that the Godhead consists of three separate and distinct personages—two Gods to bear witness of the third. Thus Christ explained: "I bear record of the Father, and the Father beareth record of me, and the Holy Ghost beareth record of the Father and me." (3 Nephi 11:32.)

It was absolutely essential that Christ comply with this principle in his mortal ministry. Had he failed to do so, none would be obligated to accept his claim to Messiahship. Knowing this, the Pharisees came to him saying, "Thou bearest record of thyself; thy record is not true" (John 8:13). Responding to their challenge, Jesus replied: "I am not alone, but I and the Father that sent me. It is also written in your law, that the testimony of two men is true. I am one that bear witness of myself, and the Father that sent me beareth witness of me." (John 8:16–18.) If the Father and the Son are not separate and distinct and are not both men, no sense can be made of the text and Christ had not responded to the challenge of his adversaries. Thus the testimony of two men, the Father and the Son, was necessary to establish to the Jews of his day the Messiahship of Christ.

As with Christ, so with his prophets. As his testimony was not to stand alone, neither is theirs; they too must comply with the laws of heaven. Thus it is that when the priesthood or its keys were restored to Joseph Smith he could not be alone. Oliver Cowdery was his companion when John the Baptist restored the Aaronic Priesthood and its keys, when Peter, James, and John restored the Melchizedek Priesthood and its keys, and when divers angels restored the authority peculiar to their ministries (D&C 2; 27:12; 110:11–16; 128:20–22). In like manner, Peter, to whom Christ promised the keys of the kingdom, received them in company with James and John on the Mount of Transfiguration (Matthew 17:1–11).[10] Having clearly established the pattern of two or more witnesses as essential to the restoration of priesthood and keys in both the meridian dispensation and this the final dispensation, we may reasonably assume that such was the pattern in Old Testament times also. In fact, it is in the Old Testament that we first learn of the law of witnesses—in that case, witnesses to an accused person's iniquitous acts (Deuteronomy 17:6; 19:15).

An attendant principle is that of the conferral of priesthood by the laying on of hands. It is apparent that from the beginning of earth's history this identifiable and documentable event has always been associated with the conferral of priesthood and that there are not and never have been any secret lines of priesthood authority. Teaching this principle in our day, the Lord said: "It shall not be given to any one to go forth to preach my gospel, or to build up my church, except he be ordained by some one who has authority, and it is known to the church that he has authority and has been regularly ordained by the heads of the church" (D&C 42:11).

Spiritual Laws

The Lord's house is a house of order. In it laws exist by which the legitimacy of all things can be tested. There are no archaic laws in the kingdom of God. The principles by which prophets are to be discerned remain the same in all dispensations, as do all the principles and doctrines of salvation. "For do we not read that God is the same yesterday, today, and forever, and in him there is no variableness neither shadow of changing?" (Mormon 9:9.) Those immutable laws embrace the following:

It is the Lord's Church and he runs it. It is for the Lord to choose his prophets and spokesmen, his ministers and priests. No one has the right to choose to so serve, any more than he has the right to dictate the terms of his salvation. It is not for man to seek to counsel his God. All calls and doctrines must be born of revelation. It is a contradiction in terms for someone to profess to have been called of God and deny at the same time the principle of revelation. When revelation ceases, calls cease; the ordinances of salvation can no longer be performed, and the doctrines of salvation can no longer be taught. All of this is a simple manifestation of the verity that it is the Lord's Church and he runs it.

As all truths are in harmony with each other, so all prophetic acts are harmonious. There is a unity and brotherhood among prophets that spans all ages. All prophets teach righteousness and testify of Christ. All prophets comply with and teach others to comply with the ordinances of salvation. True prophets are always found sustaining and supporting each other. There is not one quorum for the prophets of one age and another quorum for the prophets of another. The prophets of all ages sit side by side, so to speak; they share the same priesthood, the same ministry, and the same message. Their testimony is one. In the full and proper sense we do not have "greater prophets" and "lesser prophets" in the Old Testament, and it is but an artificial line of man's making that divides the prophets of the Old Testament or Covenant from those of the New, for there is but one covenant or plan of salvation and one message.

Having established his Church or earthly kingdom among men and having called and ordained its officers, the God of heaven respects that organization and those who function in righteousness within it. As long as that organization stands, all others are without the right or authority to represent the will of heaven, teach its doctrines, or perform its ordinances. "There is never but one on the earth at a time on whom *this* power and the keys of *this* priesthood are conferred" (D&C 132:7, italics added).

The Church can have but one earthly head. It cannot be led by discordant voices. There is but one path and one plan that leads to the divine presence. As Paul said: "The spirits of the prophets are subject to the prophets. For God is not the author of confusion, but of peace, as in all churches of the saints." (1 Corinthians 14:31–32.) That is to say that all who possess the spirit of prophecy will teach and do that which all prophets have taught and done. "It shall not be given to any one to go forth to preach my gospel," the Lord said, "or to build up my church, except he be ordained by some one who has authority, and it is known to the church that he has authority and has been regularly ordained by the heads of the church'' (D&C 42:11).

Individuals may err, prophets are not infallible, yet we have the assurance of heaven that the united voice of these chosen servants will never be allowed to lead the Church or the people of God astray. As Moses was a prophet, so was Balaam; as Peter was an apostle, so was Judas; as Joseph Smith saw the heavens opened, so did Sidney Rigdon. Though men may fall short of what they ought to be, we have the assurance that "the works, and the designs, and the purposes of God cannot be frustrated, neither can they come to naught" (D&C 3:1). "I say to Israel, the Lord will never permit me or any other man who stands as president of this Church to lead you astray," said President Wilford Woodruff. "It is not in the mind of God. If I were to attempt that the Lord would remove me out of my place, and so he will any other man who attempts to lead the children of men astray from the oracles of God and from their duty."[11] Teaching this same principle, President Joseph F. Smith said, "I testify in the name of Israel's God that He will not suffer the head of the Church, him whom He has chosen to stand at the head, to transgress His laws and apostatize; the moment he should take a course that would in time lead to it, God would take him away. Why? Because to suffer a wicked man to occupy that position, would be to allow, as it were, the fountain to become corrupted, which is something He will never permit."[12]

In the course of the Church's history some have been and others yet will be deceived by false spirits. The pattern seems to consist of their becoming convinced that something is wrong with the Church, and that they are specially chosen to set the matter right. Nothing could be more inconsistent than the supposition that, after God has called a man and appointed him to do a work and the man remains faithful, God would then bypass that man and go to someone else to have him accomplish the same purpose. Joseph F. Smith suggested that "to seriously contemplate any such idea would be charging the Almighty with inconsistency, and with being the author of confusion, discord, and schism. The kingdom of God never could be established on earth in any such way."[13]

The matter of charting and steering the course for the good ship Zion is the business of the ship's captain and those that he, and he alone, shall appoint. Nothing would be more ridiculous than to suppose that by taking passage on a ship we gained the right to redirect its course at our whim, determine its speed, or relieve its officers, even though we might suppose ourselves to be more competent than the ship's crew.

The moment we look to sources other than the channels the Lord has ordained, we become a ready prey for the influences of Satan and begin to lose sight of the true order through which the kingdom of God is administered. It is inevitable that when someone rises up claiming to have received a revelation independent of the channels the Lord has ordained, and the purpose of that revelation is to set the kingdom of God in order, he or she is an impostor.

Those who go forth to represent the Lord go forth to teach and not to be taught, and that which they teach is to be that which he has put into their hands by the power of his Spirit (see D&C 42:14). "The anointing which ye have received of [the Lord] abideth in you," John declared," and ye need not that any man teach you: but as the same anointing teacheth you of all things," so you shall teach others (1 John 2:27). Of Christ, who is our example in all things, the holy writ attests: "He spake not as other men, neither could he be taught; for he needed not that any man should teach him" (JST, Matthew 3:25).

It is an unholy alliance in which the world and its wisdom is sought to give direction to the kingdom of God. It is not for unholy men to give direction to holy causes.

The true prophet will never be found seeking to exalt himself above those he has been called to lead. There is perfect equality in the kingdom of God. No aristocracy exists in the realm of spiritual things. God, we have been assured, is no respecter of persons, neither are his prophets. All have equal claim upon the love of their divine Father. All are entitled to the fulness of gospel blessings, all make the same covenants of salvation, and all have received the same promises of eternal reward. We do not have one heaven for prophets and another for the rest of the Saints. "He that receiveth a prophet in the name of a prophet shall receive a prophet's reward" (Matthew 10:41).

It was the doctrine of spiritual equality that Christ taught to those who sought the chief seats in the synagogue. "All ye are brethren," he said, while warning of earthly honors and titles. "Neither be ye called masters," he said, "for one is your Master, even Christ. But he that is greatest among you shall be your servant. And whosoever shall exalt himself shall be abased; and he that shall humble himself shall be exalted." (Matthew 23:8–12.)

The Divine Pattern of Discernment

The work of evil spirits was so prevalent during the period in which the theological foundations of the Church were being restored that a series of revelations was given wherein the Saints were taught the principles by which false spirits, false prophets, and false doctrines were to be discerned. Instructing the elders of the Church, the Lord said: "There are many spirits which are false spirits, which have gone forth in the earth, deceiving the world. And also Satan hath sought to deceive you, that he might overthrow you. Behold, I, the Lord, have looked upon you, and have seen abominations in the church that profess my name." (D&C 50:2–4.) Having warned that there were hypocrites in the Church, the Lord commanded that "every man beware lest he do that which is not in truth and righteousness before [Him]" (D&C 50:9).

That there might be an immutable standard of judgment in these matters, a standard by which all things might be discerned, early in our dispensation the Lord said: "I will give unto you a pattern in all things, that ye may not be deceived; for Satan is abroad in the land, and he goeth forth deceiving the nations—wherefore he that prayeth, whose spirit is contrite, the same is accepted of me if he obey mine ordinances. He that speaketh, whose spirit is contrite, whose language is meek and edifieth, the same is of God if he obey mine ordinances. And again, he that trembleth under my power shall be made strong, and shall bring forth fruits of praise and wisdom, according to the revelations and truths which I have given you. And again, he that is overcome and bringeth not forth fruits, even according to his pattern, is not of me. Wherefore, *by this pattern ye shall know the spirits in all cases under the whole heavens.''* (D&C 52:14–19, italics added.)

Four tests are given in this passage: first, does the one professing authority have a contrite spirit; second, is his language meek; third, is his doctrine edifying; and fourth, has he complied with or been obedient to gospel ordinances. Extremes are easily identified: Abner Hale, in James Mitchner's *Hawaii*, with his puritanical and studied piety; the bombastic and vehement diatribe of the old circuit-riding revivalists; the hell fire and damnation of Jonathan Edwards; or the theatrics and showmanship of television evangelists—these immediately come to mind. Doctrines and deportment that do not edify are readily seen among cultists whose arguments about secret lines of authority and whose arrogated calls to "set in order the house of God" are used as a cover to hide illicit sexual practices.

And what of the shaking, quaking, whirling, jumping, and other extravagances of the revival era? What of the thousands of mediums and the spirits they conjured up with their knockings, rappings, and writings? Are such activities edifying? Are these the ways in which God has chosen to enlighten the children of men? Can a God who claims his house to be a house of order be the author of such a heterogeneous mass of confusion?

To edify means to enlighten, or to uplift through beneficial instruction or example. Well might we ask what intelligence has been communicated for the benefit of man through such activities as those just mentioned. The sum of the intelligence obtained from the revival era consisted of shouts of "Glory!," "Hallelujah!," or some incoherent expression. No visions, revelations, or commandments were received. In a like manner, the great wave of spiritualism that followed in the wake of the revivals has added nothing to our knowledge of eternal truths. Commenting on this era, Joseph F. Smith said, "I have yet to learn that a single principle has been developed from this source that will save mankind, or exalt them to the presence and glory of God."[14]

Not all delusions come in such obvious extremes. Among the legions of the adversary are bright and dull-witted devils; hell hounds and those who conduct themselves as perfect gentlemen; ignorant devils and educated devils, crude devils and urbane and sophisticated devils. How then is one to detect deception when it comes clothed in the best of taste and exhibiting the finest of manners and conduct? The key or "pattern in all things" is contrition, and obedience to gospel ordinances. Devils and their companions have a hard time keeping the Lord's commandments.

Latter-day Saints generally think of ordinances as rites or rituals like baptism and marriage. In fact, as used in scriptural texts the word *ordinance* is virtually always used as a synonym for laws or statutes. Thus, to keep the "ordinances" is to obey the law of the gospel, that is, to live in harmony with the commandments God has given. This embraces willing compliance with such rituals as baptism, receiving the Holy Ghost by the laying on of hands, and proper ordination to the priesthood, but it reaches beyond ritual observance to keeping in letter and spirit all the commandments God has given.

Conclusions

1. We accept or reject the prophets of God at the peril of our eternal lives. To accept false prophets in the name of true prophets, no matter how well intended we may be, is to refuse those ordinances and that instruction by which salvation comes. To anoint ourselves with lye thinking it to be the balm of Gilead heals no wounds.

2. The world is full of false prophets and false ideas relative to the doctrines of salvation. Phony standards for the discerning of prophets have produced the expected phony results. Yet even scriptural tests will not exceed in value the spiritual integrity of those using them. No source is misquoted or misused as often as holy writ. Devils quote scripture as often as do Saints.

3. Though many discordant voices vie for our attention, though the world is full of synthetics and counterfeits, we need not be deceived. We can discern spirits and do so with perfect confidence. As there are laws of nature, so there are spiritual laws. These laws of theology, these eternal absolutes, have been given to protect us from untruth in its variety of forms. Indeed, the Lord has given us a test or a pattern in all things, a test that has equal respect for the great and the small, a test by which we can discern in "all cases under the whole heavens." What then is that test? Simply that good seeds bring forth good fruits; that eternal principles bring forth eternal blessings; that heaven's principles require respect and obedience of their fellow principles; and that all true prophets, as with all citizens of the kingdom of God, will comply with the laws and ordinances of that kingdom, as will their message. The signs of the true messenger are faithful obedience to all that God has revealed, contrition, meekness, and a message that edifies. He will declare no doctrines or sustain no actions unworthy of God or His presence.

Notes

1. *Teachings*, p. 365.
2. *Teachings*, p. 365.
3. Martin, *The New Cults*, pp. 17–21.
4. Arrington, *Brigham Young: American Moses*, p. 75.
5. Joseph Fielding Smith, *Life of Joseph F. Smith*, p. 184.
6. Whitney, *Life of Heber C. Kimball*, p. 104.
7. Esplin, "A Great Work Done in That Land," *Ensign*, July 1987, p. 25.

8. Staniforth, *Early Christian Writings—The Apostolic Fathers*, p. 233.
9. *Teachings*, p. 278.
10. *Teachings*, p. 158.
11. Woodruff, *The Discourses of Wilford Woodruff*, pp. 212–13.
12. *Journal of Discourses*, 24:192.
13. *Journal of Discourses*, 24:189.
14. *Journal of Discourses*, 19:196.

5

> *Would God that all the Lord's people were prophets, and that the Lord would put his spirit upon them!*
> —Numbers 11:29

That All Might Be Prophets

Our faith and our doctrine is that every member of the Church has both the ability and responsibility to be a prophet. To join the Church is but to enroll in the school of the prophets. Critics of the Church foolishly suggest that its leaders seek power and authority over the membership. Yet in no other Church is every worthy male granted the right to hold the priesthood, the very power by which the ordinances of salvation come. In no other Church is every man and woman invited to participate in sacred ordinances wherein they are endowed with power from on high, including the promise that they may receive the fulness of the Father so that they might be equal with him in power, might, and dominion. All who have been baptized into the Church have had hands laid upon their heads and been given the right to the companionship of the Holy Ghost. With that companionship comes the spirit of revelation, for as the Prophet said, "No man can receive the Holy Ghost without receiving revelations" (*Teachings*, p. 328).

Our doctrine is not simply that if we live righteously we can receive revelation; rather it is that if we live right there is no power that can prevent our receiving it. Nephi declared it thus: "If ye will enter in by the way, and receive the Holy Ghost, *it will* show unto you all things what ye should do" (2

Nephi 32:5, italics added). Similarly, Joseph Smith asked, "What power shall stay the heavens?" Then he responded, "As well might man stretch forth his puny arm to stop the Missouri river in its decreed course, or to turn it up stream, as to hinder the Almighty from pouring down knowledge from heaven upon the heads of the Latter-day Saints" (D&C 121:33).

The promise of the heavens is that if we keep the commandments we will be granted truth and light until we are "glorified in truth" and come to a knowledge of all things (D&C 93:28). Such knowledge cannot be had independent of revelation—it must come to the Church by revelation and it must come to the understanding of each individual by the same source. Teaching this principle, the Lord said: "If it be some other way it is not of God" (D&C 50:18, 20). This, in the context of our present discussion, leads to the simple conclusion that all who would lay claim to the promise of salvation must do so as prophets or prophetesses. Each must claim a personal dispensation of the gospel. All who profess a testimony of the gospel must have a knowledge of saving truths that stands independent of the revelations given to others.

Adam and His Righteous Posterity Were Prophets

The first of earth's prophets was father Adam. The first of its prophetesses was mother Eve. In the *Lectures on Faith* Joseph Smith tells us that "no sooner was the plan of redemption revealed to man, and he began to call upon God, than the Holy Spirit was given, bearing record of the Father and Son" (*Lectures on Faith* 2:25). "The Holy Ghost fell upon Adam," we are told, and he "began to prophesy concerning all the families of the earth, saying: Blessed be the name of God, for because of my transgression my eyes are opened, and in this life I shall have joy, and again in the flesh I shall see God." By the same spirit Eve gave utterance to one of the most perceptive expressions of the plan of salvation ever made. "Were it not for our transgression," she declared, "we never should have had seed, and never should have known good and evil, and the joy of our redemption, and the eternal life which God giveth unto all the obedient." Adam and Eve praised God "and they made all things known unto their sons and their daughters. . . . And the Lord God called upon men by the Holy Ghost everywhere and commanded them that they should repent." (Moses 5:9–12, 14.)

Three years previous to his death Adam called a great conference of the Church in the valley of Adam-ondi-Ahman. All of Adam's righteous posterity assembled to hear the words of their aged progenitor. The Lord himself "appeared unto them, and they rose up and blessed Adam, and called him Michael, the prince, the archangel. And the Lord administered comfort unto Adam, and said unto him: I have set thee to be at the head; a multitude of nations shall come of thee, and thou art a prince over them forever. And Adam stood up in the midst of the congregation; and, not withstanding he was bowed down with age, being full of the Holy Ghost, predicted whatsoever should befall his posterity unto the latest generation." (D&C 107:53–56.)

This sacred meeting was a type and a shadow of an even greater meeting yet to be held in Adam-ondi-Ahman for Adam's righteous posterity (see D&C 116). As the faithful of Adam's family assembled anciently in the presence of the Lord, so will they assemble once again as part of the great winding-up scene of earth's mortal history. That enjoyed by the faithful of Adam's children anciently is to be enjoyed by his faithful children at the end of time also. Such was his prophecy. (Moses 6:6–7; D&C 27:5–14.)

The manner in which the heavens were opened and the Lord manifested himself in the past is but the pattern. As God revealed himself to Adam, so he would reveal himself to Adam's sons. "And they [Adam's righteous sons] were preachers of righteousness, and spake and prophesied, and called upon all men, everywhere, to repent; and faith was taught unto the children of men" (Moses 6:23).

The Order of the Church in the Days of Melchizedek and Abraham

Modern revelation affirms that where the Church was found, there the priesthood was to be found also (D&C 84:17; 107:4). Until the days of Moses, that priesthood could be held by all worthy Israelite males. As to the nature of the priesthood, we read that God "swore unto Enoch and unto his seed with an oath by himself; that every one being ordained after this order and calling should have power, by faith, to break mountains, to divide the seas, to dry up waters, to turn them out of their course; to put at defiance the armies of nations, to divide the earth, to break every band, to stand in the presence of God; to do all things according to his will, according to his command, subdue principalities and powers; and this by the will of the Son of God which was from before the foundation of the world. And men having his faith, coming up unto this order of God, were translated and taken up into heaven." (JST, Genesis 14:30–32.)

We cannot claim less for the priesthood in our day. If the priesthood does not have the power to do all that it did in the days of Enoch or Melchizedek we can hardly claim that it is the same priesthood. Our testimony to all the world is that it is the same. "The power and authority of the higher, or Melchizedek Priesthood," the Lord told Joseph Smith, "is to hold the keys of all the spiritual blessings of the church—to have the privilege of receiving the mysteries of the kingdom of heaven, to have the heavens opened unto them, to commune with the general assembly and church of the Firstborn, and to enjoy the communion and presence of God the Father, and Jesus the mediator of the new covenant" (D&C 107:18–19).

Surely a man who has been granted the authority to obtain the mysteries of heaven, have the heavens opened to him, commune with angels, and stand in the presence of the Father and the Son can, assuming he lives worthy of his ordination, profess to be nothing less than a prophet. By its very nature the priesthood makes prophets of all "men having this faith" who hold and honor it.

Israel Chosen to be a Nation of Prophets and Priests

The establishment of the nation of Israel in the days of Moses provides a perfect case study as to what the Lord desires of his people. When Moses ascended Sinai, the Lord told him to tell the children of Israel this: "If ye will obey my voice indeed, and keep my covenant, then ye shall be a peculiar treasure unto me above all people: for all the earth is mine: and ye shall be unto me a kingdom of priests, and an holy nation." Moses was then sent to sanctify his people so that they—the entire nation, men, women, and children—might stand in the presence of the Lord and behold his face. (Exodus 19:5–6, 10–11.) Had Israel lived worthy of that privilege, they would most assuredly have been "a peculiar treasure" and a "holy nation," for each of their number would have been a special witness of God. They would, in effect, have been a nation of prophets and prophetesses. But they chose otherwise.

From modern revelation we learn that Moses "sought diligently to sanctify his people that they might behold the face of God; but they hardened their hearts and could not endure his presence; therefore, the Lord in his wrath, for his anger was kindled against them, swore that they should not enter into his rest while in the wilderness, which rest is the fulness of his glory. Therefore, he took Moses out of their midst, and the Holy Priesthood also." (D&C 84:23–25.) After Moses, in his bitter disappointment, broke the tablets upon which the covenant of the Lord had been written, he returned again to the presence of the Lord to receive a law of carnal commandments. Restored texts recount the matter thus:

> And the Lord said unto Moses, Hew thee two other tablets of stone, like unto the first, and I will

write upon them also, the words of the law, according as they were written at the first on the tablets which thou brakest; but it shall not be according to the first, for I will take away the priesthood out of their midst; therefore my holy order, and the ordinances thereof, shall not go before them; for my presence shall not go up in their midst, lest I destroy them.

But I will give unto them the law as at the first, but it shall be after the law of a carnal commandment; for I have sworn in my wrath, that they shall not enter into my presence, into my rest, in the days of their pilgrimage. (JST, Exodus 34:1–2.)

Thus the Lord, always willing to grant that which men are willing to receive, gave Israel the lesser or Aaronic Priesthood with its attendant promise of the ministering of angels, while the higher priesthood, which would have brought them into his presence, was taken from them.

Moses and the Melchizedek Priesthood were not taken immediately from the people. Moses continued to minister among them until the end of the wilderness wanderings. As to the higher priesthood, it would always be held by the prophets[1] but would no longer be granted to men generally as it had been from the days of Adam to Abraham. We know, for instance, that the Lord directed Moses to assemble the seventy elders of Israel in the tabernacle so that he could come among them and grant them the spirit of prophecy. Of that occasion we are told that the Lord took that spirit that was upon Moses and placed it upon the seventy elders of Israel, and that "when the spirit rested upon them, they prophesied, and did not cease." Two of their number, Eldad and Medad by name, remained in the camp of Israel, where they also prophesied. When a report of this was brought to Moses, Joshua, then a servant of Moses, said, "My lord Moses, forbid them." Moses, masterfully capturing the teaching moment, responded: "Enviest thou for my sake? would God that all the Lord's people were prophets, and that the Lord would put his spirit upon them!" (Numbers 11:24–29.)

The Promise of Another Comforter

As the Last Supper drew to a close and Christ concluded the instruction to his chosen Apostles, he granted them the promise that after his departure they would enjoy the companionship of the Holy Ghost. The Holy Ghost, he promised, would not only bring his teachings to their remembrance but would also reveal "all things" to them (John 14:26). He also promised them another Comforter. "I will come to you. Yet a little while, and the world seeth me no more; but ye see me: because I live, ye shall live also." Indeed, he promised that he and his Father would come and take up their abode with all who loved him and kept the commandments. (John 14:16–23.) The scriptures declare to us that the "appearing of the Father and the Son" in this promise "is a personal appearance; and the idea that the Father and the Son dwell in a man's heart is an old sectarian notion, and is false" (D&C 130:3).

What then is this second comforter? Joseph Smith explained it thus:

> It is no more nor less than the Lord Jesus Christ Himself; and this is the sum and substance of the whole matter; that when any man obtains this last Comforter, he will have the personage of Jesus Christ to attend him, or appear unto him from time to time, and even He will manifest the Father unto him, and they will take up their abode with him, and the visions of the heavens will be opened unto him, and the Lord will teach him face to face, and he may have a perfect knowledge of the mysteries of the Kingdom of God; and this is the state and place the ancient Saints arrived at when they had such glorious visions— Isaiah, Ezekiel, John upon the Isle of Patmos, St. Paul in the three heavens, and all the Saints who held communion with the general assembly and Church of the Firstborn.[2]

Thus we see Christ extending to the faithful of his dispensation the same challenge and promise that was extended to the nation of Israel through Moses and that was enjoyed by many in the days of Adam, Enoch, and Melchizedek.

Paul and the Doctrine of Prophets

"Desire spiritual gifts," Paul advised the Corinthian Saints, "but rather that ye may prophesy" (1 Corinthians 14:1). An appropriate interpretive translation of this verse reads: "The highest gift you can wish for is to be able to speak the messages of God" (Phillips Modern English). As we believe that a man must be called of God by prophecy in order to preach the gospel (Articles of Faith 1:5), so we believe that he must preach by the spirit of prophecy in order that his teachings be efficacious. Continuing, Paul said, "He that prophesieth speaketh unto men to edification, and exhortation, and comfort" (verse 3). Doctrines that are born of the Spirit will enlighten, exalt, and bring peace to the soul. As all things produce after their own kind, such doctrines can come only from those who enjoy that Spirit.

As to speaking in tongues, Paul continued: "I would that ye all spake with tongues, but rather that ye prophesied: for greater is he that prophesieth than he that speaketh with tongues, except he interpret, that the church may receive edifying." Plainly, Paul felt that as it was the right for all the Saints to speak in tongues, so it was their right to enjoy the spirit of prophecy. Indeed, he reasoned that there could be no value in speaking in tongues save it was attended by the spirit of revelation and prophecy. If an investigator came to one of their meetings and they all spoke in tongues, he would think them mad, Paul said. But if they "all prophesy" he would be "convinced of all." (Verses 5–6, 23–24.)

Paul's doctrine was that when the Saints met together each was to share the fruits of his spiritual gifts. One could come having written an inspired hymn, another with doctrinal understanding, another speaking in tongues, another to interpret, and still another with the spirit of revelation; "all things [to] be done unto edifying" (verse 26). "For ye may all prophesy one by one," Paul declared, "that all may learn, and all may be comforted" (verse 31). All are to be edified of all, our modern revelation states "that every man may have an equal privilege" (D&C 88:122). "And the spirits of the prophets are subject to the prophets," Paul said (verse 32). That is, the doctrine espoused by any who truly have the spirit of prophecy will be in harmony with that doctrine revealed through those whose office it is to officially establish the doctrines of the kingdom.

By way of illustration, Paul's epistle is regarded as scripture, having come from one whose office and calling as an Apostle granted him the right to speak to the Corinthian Saints as one having authority. In turn each member of the Church in Corinth was entitled to that same spirit of prophecy that they might edify each other. In doing so they would teach no doctrines that were out of harmony with the inspired counsel or holy writ they had already received. Still they neither individually nor collectively had the authority to write an epistle of instruction to Paul or to some other branch of the Church. Thus their spirit of prophecy was subject to the prophets who had been called of the Lord to preside over them.

Concluding his thought, Paul said, "Wherefore, brethren, covet to prophesy, and forbid not to speak with tongues [nor, it might be added, forbid the expression of any other spiritual gift]. Let all things be done decently and in order" (Verses 39–40).

The Nephites and the Doctrine of Prophecy and Revelation

The doctrine that all men ought to be prophets is nowhere more plainly taught than in the Book of Mormon. Nephi introduces the record with an account of a marvelous vision vouchsafed to his father, Lehi. Having done so he then expresses his desire to drink at the fountain from which his father drank. "I, Nephi, was desirous also that I might see, and hear, and know of these things, by the power of the

Holy Ghost, which is the gift of God unto all those who diligently seek him, as well in times of old as in the time that he should manifest himself unto the children of men," he reasoned. Then, after testifying that God is the same yesterday, today, and forever, Nephi wrote of the principles that led him to seek and receive the same vision that his father had received: "He that diligently seeketh shall find; and the mysteries of God shall be unfolded unto them, by the power of the Holy Ghost, as well in these times as in times of old, and as well in times of old as in times to come; wherefore, the course of the Lord is one eternal round." (1 Nephi 10:17–19.)

To illustrate Nephi's thesis, let us take the ministering of angels, that being a rather dramatic form of revelation. Alma declared that God "imparteth his word by angels unto men, yea, not only men but women also. Now this is not all; little children do have words given unto them many times, which confound the wise and the learned." (Alma 32:23.) "Is it not as easy at this time for the Lord to send his angel . . . ," Alma asks, "as after the time of his coming?" (Alma 39:19.) Similarly, Mormon inquires: "Have angels ceased to appear unto the children of men? Or has he withheld the power of the Holy Ghost from them? Or will he, so long as time shall last, or the earth shall stand, or there shall be one man upon the face thereof to be saved? Behold I say unto you, Nay; for it is by faith that miracles are wrought; and it is by faith that angels appear and minister unto men; wherefore, if these things have ceased wo be unto the children of men, for it is because of unbelief, and all is vain." (Moroni 7:36–37.)

Restoration of the Spirit of Revelation

With the restoration of the Melchizedek Priesthood in the present dispensation came that authority by which the gift of the Holy Ghost is conferred upon those who have been properly baptized and confirmed members of the Church (see Joseph Smith—History 1:70; D&C 49:14). To restore the authority to confer the Holy Ghost is to restore the gift of revelation, for as we have already noted, to receive the Holy Ghost is to receive revelation, for the Holy Ghost is a revelator.[3] If priesthood is the authority to act in the name of God, a person can hardly claim to exercise the priesthood save he does so by the spirit of revelation. The claim to represent God rings very hollow if that person's God will not speak to him.

As to the importance of the Holy Ghost, the Prophet explained:

> No man can be called to fill any office in the ministry without it; we also believe in prophecy, in tongues, in visions, and in revelations, in gifts, and in healings; and that these things cannot be enjoyed without the gift of the Holy Ghost. We believe that the holy men of old spake as they were moved by the Holy Ghost, and that holy men in these days speak by the same principle; we believe in its being a comforter and a witness bearer, that it brings things past to our remembrance, leads us into all truth, and shows us of things to come; we believe that 'no man can know that Jesus is the Christ, but by the Holy Ghost.'[4]

Restoring a Nation of Prophets and Priests

In the revelation given as a preface to the Doctrine and Covenants the Lord declares that the gospel is being restored so that men should not trust in the arm of flesh, "but that every man might speak in the name of God the Lord, even the Savior of the world" (D&C 1:19–20). With the restoration of the Melchizedek Priesthood came the "key of the mysteries of the kingdom, even the key of the knowledge of God" (D&C 84:19). To have and use such keys is to have the heavens opened, to commune with heavenly beings, and to enjoy the actual presence of the Father and the Son (see D&C 107:19). Indeed, the Lord has established the kingdom that he sought to establish in the days of Moses—a nation of prophets and priests.

Elder Bruce R. McConkie wrote: "Holders of the Melchizedek Priesthood have power to press forward in righteousness, living by every word that proceedeth forth from the mouth of God, magnifying their callings, going from grace to grace, until through the fulness of the ordinances of the temple they receive the fulness of the priesthood and are ordained kings and priests. Those so attaining shall have exaltation and be kings, priests, rulers, and lords in their respective spheres in the eternal kingdoms of the great King who is God our Father."[5] John wrote of those of the meridian Church who would attain that status (Revelation 1:5–6), and prophesied that in the last days there would be those from among every kindred, tongue, people, and nation who would obtain like blessings (Revelation 5:9–10).

Conclusions

1. It is fundamental to the testimony of all professing Christians that the righteous prophets, priests, and kings among the nation of Israel were types—that is, living prophecies for their own people—of their promised Messiah. All agree that Christ was the great Prophet, Priest, and King. Nor could any professing Christian dispute that Christ is the prototype or standard of salvation.[6] Indeed, salvation consists of our becoming like him. Now, if we are to be saved by becoming Christlike, can we reason other than that the process of salvation requires of every man that he become a prophet, priest, and king; and that every woman become a prophetess, priestess, and queen? Surely there can be no salvation in the kingdom of heaven for any accountable soul independent of their obtaining the spirit of prophecy and revelation.

2. Moses, seeking a point of illustration by which he could depict the promised Messiah in such a manner that the faithful in Israel could recognize him with perfect assurance, said he would be "like unto me" (Deuteronomy 18:15). The comparison was bold, graphic, and entirely appropriate. By

comparing himself to Christ, Moses captured what might be called the doctrine of prophets or the very doctrine of salvation itself. Salvation is obtained by our taking upon us the name of Christ and then, as already observed, doing the things that Christ did to obtain his salvation. Moses was a similitude of Christ for his generation as all prophets represent Christ to those over whom they have been called to preside. All prophets who lived before the coming of Christ were to be types and shadows of what Christ would be. In like manner, all prophets living after the ministry of Christ were or are to be types of the Christ. As this principle is true of prophets, so it is true of all who hope to obtain life eternal. Simply stated, salvation is obtained by becoming as Christ is and in no other way. Only to the extent that we have come to believe and do as he believed and did have we worked out our salvation. All who desire salvation ought to be seeking to become living prophecies of the nature of Christ; they ought to be striving to be in his image and likeness, and one ought to be able to say of them that they are, as Moses was, "like unto him."

3. All prophets are like Christ to a greater or lesser degree. We conclude that as Christ is our exemplar, so are those who have been ordained to the prophetic office. In turn, those ordained to that office are but the pattern of what every elder and sister in Israel ought to be. Thus the words of Moses echo down through the ages: "Would God that all the Lord's people were prophets!" Assuredly we ought to be!

Notes

1. *Teachings*, p. 181.
2. *Teachings*, pp. 150–51.
3. *Teachings*, p. 328.
4. *Teachings*, p. 243.
5. Bruce R. McConkie, *Mormon Doctrine*, p. 425.
6. *Lectures on Faith*, 7:9.

Prophecy

6

For the testimony of Jesus is the spirit of prophecy.
—Revelation 19:10

The Need for Prophecy

It was the hope of Caiaphas and the Sanhedrin that the death of Christ would bring with it the demise of the Nazarene's influence and the end of the Church he had organized. But meridian Christianity did not die with Christ; rather, it flourished in a great outpouring of the spirit of prophecy and revelation which spread throughout all the world.[1] The death of the Church came only with the death of prophets and prophecy. "The fate of the vast majority of Christians was not to be overcome by a frontal attack—true martyrs were relatively few—but to be led astray by perverters. The spoilers do not destroy the vineyard, but 'seize the inheritance' for themselves; we read of betrayal, disobedience, corruptions, of deceivers, perverters, traitors, or wresting the Scriptures, denying the gifts, quenching the spirit, turning love into hate, truth to fables, sheep to wolves, of embracing 'another gospel'; and so forth. The offenders are not pagans but loudly professing Christians. As, once the prophets are dead, everyone paints their tombs with protestations of devotion, so, 'when the master of the house has risen up and shut the door,' shall the eager host apply for admission to his company—too late."[2] What we witness in that which is now called historical Christianity was the substitution of erudition for inspiration, and rhetoric for revelation. To be sure, the Church organized by Christ was not deserted—it was perverted, as scholarship supplanted seership and a closed canon replaced the once-opened heavens.[3]

We Cannot Live on Borrowed Light

Thomas Paine, whose pamphlet *Common Sense* so articulately defended the need for a revolution to free the American people from the oppressive dominion of Britain and the Old World, held that "a revolution in the system of government would be followed by a revolution in the system of religion." To that end he set his powerful pen to work composing another classic, *The Age of Reason*, in which he marshaled an impressive array of arguments against the religions of the day. "All national institutions of churches, whether Jewish, Christian, or Turkish, appear to me no other than human inventions, set up to terrify and enslave mankind, and monopolize power and profit," he began. Paine described this union of church and state as an "adulterous connection," and centered his attack on what we might call the revelation heresy". Each of these churches shows certain book," he noted, "which they call 'revelation,' or the word of God. The Jews say that their word of God was given by God to Moses, face to face; the Christians say their word of God came by divine inspiration; and the Turks say that their word of God (the Koran) was brought by an angel from heaven." The issue was which if any of them constituted true revelation. Paine held that none did.

Revelation, Paine argued, must be *immediate* communication from God to man.

> No one will deny or dispute the power of the Almighty to make such a communication, if he pleases. But admitting, for the sake of a case, that something has been revealed to a certain person, and not revealed to any other person, it is revelation to that person only. When he tells it to a second person, a second to a third, a third to a fourth, and so on, it ceases to be a revelation to all those persons. It is a revelation to the

first person only, and a *hearsay* to every other, and consequently they are not obliged to believe it.

It is a contradiction in terms and ideas to call anything a revelation that comes to us at second hand, either verbally or in writing. Revelation is necessarily limited to the first communication—after this, it is only an account of something which that person says was a revelation made to him; and though he may find himself obliged to believe it, it cannot be incumbent on me to believe it in the same manner, for it was not a revelation made to *me*, and I have only his word for it that it was made to him.[4]

Paine's argument is a legitimate extension of the theme that a God who is no respecter of persons and who has revealed something to one man is obligated to reveal the same thing to all men, according to the same principles by which he revealed it to the first. "A thing which everybody is required to believe requires that the proof and evidence of it should be equal to all and universal," he properly held.[5] In its essential elements Paine's argument is absolutely correct. Without revelation, without the spirit of prophecy, without the Holy Ghost, there is no true religion. When religionists of all varieties claim allegiance to dead prophets and reverence for the revelations given to another people in another day, they are seeking salvation in the works of others—claiming *their* prophets, *their* promises, and *their* faith, as if their baptism would remit our sins and their ordination confer authority upon us.

Only the opening of the heavens can adequately respond to the charge of a second-hand or hearsay religion. A new dispensation of the gospel is needed, including a complete restoration of its doctrines, its priesthood, and its ordinances. The ancient order must be restored, including apostles, prophets, the gift of prophecy, and revelation. Once again, we need a people who can testify that God has spoken, does speak, and will continue to speak.

Not only is an institutional dispensation needed in which the principles and practices of the primitive Church are restored, but individual dispensations are also needed. It is not required that every doctrine and practice of the Church be restored on an individual basis to every man, woman, and child, but it is required that each of them know of the truthfulness of those doctrines and practices by personal revelation. No one can be dependent on another for a knowledge and testimony of the gospel. Come the day of judgment, each stands alone. Everyone is personally responsible for what he chooses to believe, and equally responsible for what he chooses not to believe. No one is saved by another's faith or condemned by another's doubt.

Nowhere is the promise of personal revelation more beautifully stated than in Joseph Smith's marvelous vision of the degrees of glory. The revelation reads:

> For thus saith the Lord—I, the Lord, am merciful and gracious unto those who fear me, and delight to honor those who serve me in righteousness and in truth unto the end.
>
> Great shall be their reward and eternal shall be their glory.
>
> And to them will I reveal all mysteries, yea, all the hidden mysteries of my kingdom from days of old, and for ages to come, will I make known unto them the good pleasure of my will concerning all things pertaining to my kingdom.
>
> Yea, even the wonders of eternity shall they know, and things to come will I show them, even the things of many generations.
>
> And their wisdom shall be great, and their understanding reach to heaven; and before them the wisdom of the wise shall perish, and the understanding of the prudent shall come to naught.
>
> For by my Spirit will I enlighten them, and by my power will I make known unto them the secrets of my will—yea, even those things which eye has not seen, nor ear heard, nor yet entered into the heart of man. (D&C 76:5–10.)

The windows of heaven may be opened to all. There are no doctrines, no experiences, no knowledge in the realm of spiritual things that are the exclusive provinces of prophets. What God grants to one, he will grant to all. Spirituality, knowledge, visions, and revelations are not offices in the priesthood but rather are the rightful inheritances of those who serve God in righteousness and truth.

Prophecy and the Commission to Preach

It is fundamental to true religion that "a man must be called of God, by prophecy, and by the laying on of hands by those who are in authority, to preach the Gospel and administer in the ordinances thereof" (Articles of Faith 1:5). Men are no more at liberty to choose to represent God than they are to choose the doctrines or principles upon which salvation is predicated. No society allows one man to choose to represent another without the express consent of the one being represented. If it were for men to choose to represent God, all manner of scoundrels would do so. No occupation could possibly be more attractive to devils. Many a dark deed has been performed in the sanction of religion and the guise of piety. The religious world has never known a shortage of men who, like cowbirds, lay their eggs in the nests of others. The offspring of their deception is then found devouring the food of the rightful nestlings and thus causing their death. So false claims to the priesthood and the commission to represent God have brought spiritual starvation to the unsuspecting.

It is an eternal verity that by accepting those who truly come in the name of the Lord we have accepted the Lord; conversely, to reject those who properly come in his name is to reject him. Every accountable person makes such judgments at the peril of his or her eternal life. Such being the case, it is absolutely imperative that those professing to represent the Lord be commissioned by him in such a manner that all honest truth-seekers can know of the verity of that commission with perfect assuredness. Though the tests of discernment may be relatively sophisticated in some instances, we can be perfectly confident that anyone who cannot claim to have been called by prophecy—that is, by revelation—cannot and does not represent the God of heaven. Without the spirit of prophecy none can profess to preach, teach, or minister in the name of the Lord.

Prophecy and the Doctrines of the Gospel

All true religion is revealed religion. Either a doctrine came from God or it is not of God. Doctrines of salvation are not born in the minds of men. Any doctrine not born of the family of revelation is without authority or heirship in the kingdom of heaven. If it were in the province of the mortal mind to concoct the doctrines of salvation, we would have little need for divine intervention. If we could save ourselves without troubling God, we ought to do so. For that matter, if the wisdom of man were greater than that of God, it would be logical for us to invite him to serve us in the hope that he might thereby obtain a great exaltation. Surely it is but darkness and folly to suppose that for mankind there can be any source of the doctrines of salvation save the spirit of prophecy and revelation.

Prophecy and Teaching the Gospel

There is but one acceptable way to teach a revealed religion, and that is by the spirit of revelation. Of those who properly taught the gospel in times past the holy writ says: "They preached the word, and the truth, according to the spirit of prophecy and revelation; and they preached after the holy order of God by which they were called" (Alma 43:2). That we might understand that the order of God has not changed in our day the Lord asked the question of those whom he had called and commissioned to declare the message of the Restoration, "Unto what were ye ordained?" Responding to his own question, he said: "To preach my gospel by the Spirit, even the Comforter which was sent forth to teach the truth." That is, they were commissioned to teach his gospel, not one of their own devising, and they were to do it by the spirit of prophecy—i.e., the Comforter or Holy Ghost. That this all-important point not be missed, again the Lord asked: "He that is ordained of me and sent forth to preach the word of truth by the Comforter, in the Spirit of truth, doth he preach it by the Spirit of truth or some other way?" (D&C 50:13–17.)

The question assumes that nothing but truth is being taught. Truth is not the issue in this instance. The issue is *how* the truth is being taught, and the purpose for which the truth is being used, the clear intimation being that there are unacceptable ways to teach and use truth. Surely all persons of spiritual sensitivity have been offended by the self-saving testimonies of Christ that are a feature of many radio and television ministries. Heaven-sent truths have been cheapened by vain repetition, vulgarized in discordant music, robbed of their meaning as they are married to the philosophies of men, stripped of their power as they are filtered through uninspired theories of science, and perverted beyond recognition in numerous other causes.

Thus the Lord asks again, "He that is ordained of me and sent forth to preach the word of truth by the Comforter, in the Spirit of truth, doth he preach it by the Spirit of truth or some other way?" Responding again to his own question, the Lord announces, "If it be by some other way [that is, some way other than by the spirit of prophecy and revelation in which it was originally given] it is not of God." (D&C 50:17–18.)

As the gospel is ever the same, so is the manner in which it is to be taught. If it was taught to the prophets in the spirit of revelation, it is to be taught *by* the prophets in the spirit of revelation. The spirit of prophecy is no less important to the teaching of the gospel today than it was in days past. If it required the spirit of prophecy and revelation to carry the truths of the gospel to the hearts of those who listened to Christ, or those who listened to the ancient prophets or Apostles, could we not expect that it would take that same spirit to carry that same message to the hearts of those of our modern age?

Prophecy and Learning the Gospel

It was Paul who reminded the ancient Saints that as the things of man are understood by the spirit of man, so the things of God can be known only by the Spirit of God. "Now we have received, not the spirit of the world," he said, "but the spirit which is of God; that we might know the things that are freely given to us of God. Which things also we speak, not in the words which man's wisdom teacheth, but which the Holy Ghost teacheth; comparing spiritual things with spiritual. But the natural man receiveth not the things of the Spirit of God: for they are foolishness unto him: neither can he know them, because they are spiritually discerned." (1 Corinthians 2:11–14.) The gospel was not given to satisfy the need of scholars for a game of mental gymnastics, to provide philosophers with a curriculum for weighty discussions, or as a whetstone upon which hoary-headed rabbis could sharpen their wits. Faith is not a matter of intellect; righteousness is not born of scholarship; obedience and sacrifice are not the offspring of linguistic or memory skills. A gospel born of the Spirit can only be known by the Spirit.

Before the Lord would show Enoch the grand vision of earth's history, the prophet was required to "anoint" his eyes with clay and then wash them (see Moses 6:35). How perfect the lesson—if we are to see the visions of eternity, each must first wash from his eyes the temporal, the carnal, the sensual, all that is dust and mud, all that is earthly, that he might see with purer eyes. Of a similar experience Moses declared: "Mine own eyes have beheld God; but not my natural, but my spiritual eyes, for my natural eyes could not have beheld; for I should have withered and died in his presence; but his glory was upon me; and I beheld his face, for I was transfigured before him." Moses learned his lesson well, for when Satan came demanding that Moses worship him, the prophet responded: "Where is thy glory, that I should worship thee? For behold, I could not look upon God, except his glory should come upon me, and I were transfigured before him. But I can look upon thee in the natural man."

(Moses 1:11, 13–14.) As "no man has seen God at any time in the flesh, except quickened by the Spirit of God" (D&C 67:11), so no man has seen and understood the things of God save they have been quickened by that same Spirit.

The lesson is profoundly important. It is not enough to embrace truth. Truth, like everything else, needs good company to work righteousness. A devil with a Bible is a devil just the same. James said it best: "Thou believest that there is one God; thou doest well: the devils also believe, and tremble" (James 2:19). Of each that embraces the truth the question must still be asked, "Have you received it by the spirit of prophecy and revelation or some other way?" For it must be understood that "if it be some other way it is not of God." (D&C 50:19–20.) A spiritual truth taught or learned independent of the Spirit is a branch broken from the tree that gave it life. Even a branch broken from the tree of life can no longer bear fruit. A church claiming to be built on past revelation which denies modern revelation has destroyed its own foundation. As the institution or organization of the Church must be born of revelation, so the sure knowledge of the principles of which it consists must be born anew by the spirit of prophecy and revelation to each who claims citizenship in that Church. The Church is but the pattern for its members—and as it must be founded in the revealed testimony of Jesus, so must they. As it is to govern and direct its affairs by revelation, so they are to govern and direct their affairs by that same spirit. The Church is but the schoolhouse wherein the members learn to govern themselves.

It Takes Prophecy to Understand Prophecy

It took the New Testament to bring the meaning and understanding to the Old Testament. Such is the divine pattern—scripture given that we might more fully understand the scripture already given, new revelation that we might more fully understand the revelations of old. It takes prophets to understand prophets, and the spirit of prophecy to understand prophecy. To properly interpret a language one must know that language. To properly interpret revelation one must know the language of revelation. That which has been given by the Spirit can only in the complete and full sense be understood by the Spirit.

Thus as the prophets of the New Testament gave meaning to the prophecy of the Old Testament, we expect prophets of our day to give meaning to the writings of the meridian prophets. And so it is that in literally hundreds of instances the language of the Old and New Testament prophets is picked up in the revelations of our day, which explain and expound so that we might see as the prophets saw and know as they knew. Much is said by proud scholars about insights obtained by their knowledge of Hebrew, Greek, and other ancient languages that bring light to our understanding of the ancient scriptural texts. We applaud their efforts and rejoice in the increased understanding they have given us. Yet we ought not to lose sight of the fact that the original language of every revelation is the language of the Spirit, the language of the Holy Ghost, which is our only sure source of light in understanding the intent of our ancient mentors the prophets.

The Bible and all other scriptural records are but a sealed book to any who seek to understand them independent of the spirit in which they were written. The eternal verity is that those professing a sealed canon—those announcing that all necessary scripture has been given, and that God will give no more—shall have taken from them even that understanding which they have (see 2 Nephi 28:29–30). The professing Christian who refuses to admit the necessity of the spirit of revelation in understanding the New Testament will see no more of the true meaning of that book than the professing Jew can see of the true meaning and intent of the Old Testament writers. Jews who could quote and expound scripture endlessly failed to recognize the Christ when he came, because they rejected the spirit of prophecy and the responsibility to live worthy of it. Similarly, there is no shortage of Bible believers in our day who also quote and expound that book endlessly but will fail to recognize either Christ or his gospel because they too have rejected the spirit of prophecy and the necessity of living worthy of it.

Prophecy: The Source of Faith and Power

No matter how beautifully the adjectives are woven together, one cannot warm one's hands or feet by the description of a fire. The fires of testimony that gave warmth and light to the souls of the ancient Saints must be kindled anew. If we are to believe as they believed and live as they lived we must be endowed with the same blessings with which they were endowed. Such has ever been the pattern among the Lord's people. Jacob, Lehi's son, described it thus: "We search the prophets, and we have many revelations and the spirit of prophecy; and having all these witnesses we obtain a hope, and our faith becometh unshaken, insomuch that we truly can command in the name of Jesus and the very trees obey us, or the mountains, or the waves of the sea." (Jacob 4:6.)

Those of the last days are not expected to labor in the Lord's vineyard on reduced wages. The spiritual fruits of which we have been invited to partake are as sweet to the taste and as abundant in their harvest as they have ever been. Thus, being potentially equal with the ancients in knowledge and power, we can be equal with them in faith and works. Joseph Smith declared that the knowledge that God is the same yesterday, today, and forever "gives to the minds of the Latter-day Saints the same power and authority to exercise faith in God which the Former-day Saints had; so that all the saints, in this respect, have been, are, and will be, alike until the end of time; for God never changes, therefore his attributes and character remain forever the same. And as it is through the revelation of these that a foundation is laid for the exercise of faith in God unto life and salvation, the foundation, therefore, for the exercise of faith was, is, and ever will be, the same; so that all men have had, and will have, an equal privilege."[6]

Prophecy: Our Source of Inspired Direction

A prophet is first and foremost a teacher—a teacher guided by the spirit of prophecy and revelation. To prophesy is to speak the mind and will of God. It is to say and do what he would say and do in the same circumstances. Anything that is properly done in the name of Jesus Christ partakes of the spirit of prophecy. The primary form of prophecy among the Saints ought be the inspired teaching of the gospel. Our revelation declares that "whatsoever they [in the broad sense meaning any member of the Church] shall speak when moved upon by the Holy Ghost shall be scripture, shall be the will of the Lord, shall be the mind of the Lord, shall be the word of the Lord, shall be the voice of the Lord, and the power of God unto salvation" (D&C 68:4).

From some of our greatest prophets we have received no predictive declarations. Christ referred to John the Baptist as the greatest prophet born of woman, yet we have no record of his having predicted any future events. Melchizedek was a prophet of such stature that he has been honored by having the priesthood carry his name, yet the Bible contains no prophecies by him. The primary function of a prophet is to expound the word of God—it is to teach the principles of his gospel.

In addition to their primary duty as gospel teachers and special witnesses of Christ, prophets in all ages have been a source of inspired warning, consolation, and expressions of hope for the Saints of their day and world. It would seem less than appropriate for a living Church to be dependent on dead prophets to lead them. At all levels of Church government those called to lead are entitled to that portion of the spirit of prophecy essential to their stewardship.

As prophecy is necessary for the collective body of the Church, so it is necessary on an individual basis. At baptism every member of the Church is given the gift of the Holy Ghost. Those living worthy of this gift are prophets and prophetesses in their own right. By this gift they can obtain the sure knowledge of the truthfulness of the gospel, have its doctrines unfolded to their minds, and receive personal promptings by way of protection and direction.

The More Sure Word of Prophecy

> An actual knowledge to any person, that the course of life which he pursues is according to the will of God, is essentially necessary to enable him to have that confidence in God without which no person can obtain eternal life. . . . Such was, and always will be, the situation of the saints of God, that unless they have an actual knowledge that the course they are pursuing is according to the will of God they will grow weary in their minds, and faint; for such has been, and always will be, the opposition in the hearts of unbelievers and those that know not God against the pure and unadulterated religion of heaven (the only thing which insures eternal life), that they will persecute to the uttermost all that worship God according to his revelations, receive the truth in the love of it, and submit themselves to be guided and directed by his will; and drive them to such extremities that nothing short of an actual knowledge of their being the favorites of heaven, and of their having embraced the order of things which God has established for the redemption of man, will enable them to exercise that confidence in him, necessary for them to overcome the world, and obtain that crown of glory which is laid up for them that fear God.[7]

Independent of the spirit of revelation no one could have the assurance that Joseph Smith speaks of in the preceding quotation. The Apostle Peter declared the doctrine whereby a man might know that the path he was pursuing was approved by heaven as "a more sure word of prophecy" (2 Peter 1:19). "The more sure word of prophecy," Joseph Smith said, "means a man's knowing that he is sealed up into eternal life, by revelation and the spirit of prophecy through the power of the Holy Priesthood." He added that it was "impossible for a man to be saved" without such knowledge. (D&C 131:5–6.) Christ promised the meridian Saints that, subject to their keeping his commandments, after his ascension he and his Father would make their abode with them. Again by revelation in our day we are told that "the appearing of the Father and the Son, in that verse [John 14:23], is a personal appearance; and the idea that the Father and the Son dwell in a man's heart is an old sectarian notion, and is false" (D&C 130:3).

Thus the promise is to be extended to the righteous who have been married for eternity and been sealed by the Holy Spirit of promise by one of the Lord's anointed that they will "come forth in the first resurrection . . . and shall inherit thrones, kingdoms, principalities, and powers, dominions, all heights and depths . . . [and] when they are out of the world . . . they shall pass by the angels, and the gods, which are set there, to their exaltation and glory in all things, as hath been sealed upon their heads, which glory shall be a fulness and a continuation of the seeds forever and ever" (D&C 132:19).

Conclusions

1. The spirit of prophecy and revelation is the life blood of the gospel. Indeed, without it there is no gospel—for all true religion is revealed religion. Without the spirit of prophecy no one could be commissioned to teach or preach the gospel. Further, the gospel can only be properly taught by the spirit of prophecy and revelation, and it can only be properly learned when we are being tutored by that same spirit. It is the spirit of prophecy that gives life and meaning to the revelations of the past—without it our understanding of the ancient scriptural records reaches no closer to heaven than did the tower of Babel. The spirit of prophecy is the mother of faith and power; it is the parent of confidence and assurance. If we are without the spirit of prophecy we are without first-hand testimony, and without the whisperings of the Holy Ghost to comfort, protect, and direct us. And surely without the spirit of prophecy we are without the religion of

the faithful Saints of ages past. Salvation is not to be found in borrowed experiences or second-hand testimony.

2. To deny the spirit of revelation is to offend God and advocate war with the spirit of truth. "Quench not the Spirit" Paul admonished; "despise not prophesyings," he warned (1 Thessalonians 5:19–20). "Wo unto him that spurneth at the doings of the Lord," wrote Mormon; "yea, wo unto him that shall deny the Christ and his works! Yea, wo unto him that shall deny the revelations of the Lord, and that shall say the Lord no longer worketh by revelation, or by prophecy, or by gifts, or by tongues, or by healings, or by the power of the Holy Ghost!" (3 Nephi 29:5–6.) "Deny not the spirit of revelation, nor the spirit of prophecy," the Lord said to Hyrum Smith, "for wo unto him that denieth these things" (D&C 11:25). "Cursed is he," the Lord said through the pen of Nephi, "that putteth his trust in man, or maketh flesh his arm, or shall hearken unto the precepts of men, save their precepts shall be given by the power of the Holy Ghost" (2 Nephi 28:31).

Notes

1. In his great discourse on the events of the last days, Christ tells us that the gospel will once "again" be "preached in all the world." This, like the other signs cited by Christ, is a parallel or repeat of the events of the meridian dispensation. (JST, Matthew 24:32.)

2. Nibley, "The Passing of the Church," pp. 3–4.

3. "The arguments put forth by those who would prove the survival of the Church are enough in themselves to cast serious doubts upon it. The first thing that strikes one is the failure of the ingenuity of scholarship to discover any serious scriptural support for the thesis. There are remarkably few passages in the Bible that yield encouragement even to the most determined exegesis, and it is not until centuries of discussion have passed that we meet with the now familiar interpretations of the 'mustard seed' and 'gates-of-hell' imagery, which some now hold to be eschatological teachings having no reference whatever to the success of the Church on earth." (Nibley, "The Passing of the Church," p. 13.)

4. Paine, *The Age of Reason, Part 1*, pp. 4–5.
5. Paine, *The Age of Reason, Part 1*, p. 8.
6. Smith, *Lectures on Faith*, 4:19.
7. Smith, *Lectures on Faith*, 6:2, 4.

7

How Prophecy Comes

> God, who at sundry times and in divers manners spake in time past unto the fathers by the prophets, hath in these last days spoken unto us by his Son.
> —Hebrews 1:1–2

If God is "without partiality," as James attested, and he has spoken to so much as one man, he must of necessity be willing, on the same terms, to speak to all men (James 3:17). Such has ever been the testimony of those to whom he has spoken. Never have we had a prophet who said, "Having spoken to me, God will speak to none else!" Moses, who stood face to face with God, sought to have all in the nation of Israel share the same experience (Exodus 19:11; D&C 84:23). "This principle," Joseph Smith said, "ought (in its proper place) to be taught, for God hath not revealed anything to Joseph, but what He will make known unto the Twelve, and even the least Saint may know all things as fast as he is able to bear them, for the day must come when no man need say to his neighbor, Know ye the Lord; for all shall know Him (who remain) from the least to the greatest."[1]

It is a strange notion that God has the power of creation but not the power of communication. The true issue is not does God "who at sundry times and in divers manners spake in time past" still speak, but rather, what did the ancients do whereby they merited the right to hear his voice, that we might do the same? To respond to such a question we must first separate myth from truth relative to the nature of the spirit of prophecy. Having done so we can then identify its proper functions and the requisites for receiving it.

Revelation Myths

When prophecy ceases among a people, we inevitably find them professing a boundless faith in the revelations of previous generations. It has ever been the practice of those who have made a shipwreck of the plan of salvation to throw the living prophets overboard. Those rejecting Christ in his mortal ministry did so professing loyalty to the revelations of Moses. Those rejecting Joseph Smith do so professing a reverence for the prophets of the Old and New Testaments. These argue that the greatness of the Bible (that is, whatever compilation of revelations from the past suits their purposes) precludes the necessity of continued communication with the heavens. This is the dogma of sufficiency—the profession that whatever we have is all we need. One of the unavoidable effects of this closed-canon theology is that the knowledge of how revelation comes is also unavoidably lost. If we cease to plant the seeds of revelation, not only do we cease to enjoy its fruits but we also forget what the plant looked like. In the meantime the weeds of myth quickly overrun what was once a fruitful garden.

Our day has seen no shortage of critics of revelation, be it ancient or modern. Not having received the spirit of revelation, these critics refuse to entertain the possibility that others could. Their arguments evidence little more than their ignorance of that which they have not experienced. Among the myths perpetuated from such sources are the following:

Myth number one: *Revelations cannot be added to.* A popular myth in anti-Mormon literature is that once a revelation has been recorded, no additions can be made to it. In fact, it is probably more common to the spirit of revelation to reveal things in a piecemeal fashion than to do otherwise. The practice of heaven is to dispense its treasures "line upon line, precept upon precept, here a little, and there a little" (2 Nephi 28:30). It was necessary for the Son of God himself to advance in understanding from "grace to grace" (D&C 93:12–14). Indeed, it ought to be said that no revelation has ever been given that cannot be added to. The total knowledge and wisdom of God on any matter cannot be contained in any book, let alone in a single chapter, paragraph, or sentence.

When scripture is read with that Spirit by which it came, that Spirit will by its very nature take us in our understanding beyond the literal rendering of the verse or verses being read. The Spirit of the Lord expands the mind (Alma 32:34); it does not contract it. "That which is of God is light; and he that receiveth light, and continueth in God, receiveth more light; and that light groweth brighter and brighter until the perfect day" (D&C 50:24). Nothing is more in harmony with the Spirit of revelation than the expansion of or the adding to existing revelations.

Myth number two: *Revelations cannot be changed or edited.* Jehovah gave Moses the Law on Sinai. That same Jehovah, when incarnate, freely edited that law in the Sermon on the Mount. It will be remembered that he repetitiously said, "It was said by them of old time, Thou shall not do this or that; but I say unto you that thou shalt do otherwise." Such is the perogative of the Lawgiver, and such is the perogative of those he has called to be his spokesmen. "I, the Lord, command and revoke, as it seemeth me good," he said (D&C 56:4). The keys of the priesthood always embrace the power to bind and to loose both on earth and in heaven (Matthew 16:19; D&C 32:45–47).

In its common form God will plant the seed of prophecy and revelation in the heart and mind of an individual, leaving him or her with the responsibility (to the extent that it is appropriate) to clothe their heaven-sent knowledge in words. This is why the revelations and prophecies recorded in the various books of the Bible are so different in style and manner of expression; each reflects the skills of expression native to the one recording it. The process of revelation can be likened to that of an artist painting. As the artist represents with paint and brush that which his eyes have beheld, so the prophet or recipient of a revelation represents with words that which he has seen and felt. To argue that a prophet cannot edit or rewrite that which has been revealed to him to add to its clarity would be akin to arguing that an artist who touched up a painting either did not see that which he painted or was without inspiration in the first place.

Myth number three: *Revelations are inerrant and infallible.* Because a man is poorly clothed does not mean he is without inspiration. So it is with heaven-sent truths. Grammatical errors do not make a good doctrine bad any more than grammatical correctness makes a bad doctrine good. All rules of grammar are man-made. We have no revelations in which spelling or punctuation was revealed. Nor do we have any scriptural statement that sustains the idea that revelations are given in language that is perfect and final. The languages of men, all of which have their idiosyncrasies and imperfections, are woefully inadequate to do justice to the revelations of heaven. It is generally conceded that the writing of most revelations could be improved. The first seventy-five years of this century witnessed more than 150 new translations of the Bible (in whole or in part) into the English language alone.[2] Only dead languages are without change. There is no language, save the Adamic or celestial, that does not impose some limitations on the revelations of heaven.

For that matter, within the scriptures we even find the verities of heaven taught with incorrect illustrations. Moses wrote of eagles bearing their young upon their wings (Deuteronomy 32:11), something that eagles simply cannot do, though until the nineteenth century it was thought that they did. Though the illustration is faulty, its purpose, which is to illustrate God's power to bless his people, was most appropriate. A number of Old Testament writers make reference to leviathan (thought to be a many-headed, serpent-like sea monster) in contexts which do not suggest that the references are figurative (Job 41:1–10; Psalm 74:14; 104:25–27).[3] Further, it was not uncommon for Old Testament prophets to draw on pagan symbolism in scriptural texts. For instance, Isaiah uses the form of a Canaanite ritual drama in a dual prophecy which describes the fall of the king of Babylon and the ultimate defeat of Lucifer (see Isaiah 14:1–23).[4] Malachi quotes the Lord as saying that the "Sun of righteousness" will arise with healing in his wings (Malachi 4:2). The imagery "is derived from the symbolism of Egyptian religion —a symbolism also found elsewhere in the ancient Near East."[5] Paul does the same kind of thing in Athens, apparently using the words of a pagan poem to support the verity that man is the offspring of Deity (Acts 17:28). Indeed, many an inspired discourse has drawn upon illustrations that are not the equal of the eternal verities being taught.

To argue that the scriptures must be inerrant and infallible is to impose upon them a standard that they do not profess for themselves. Those so arguing as a rule admit that the scriptures contain transmissional errors while maintaining that the original manuscripts were entirely without human corruption of any sort. It is conceded, however, that there are no extant originals. One advocate of infallibility writes, "We must cherish the inerrant originals of Holy Scripture as free from all mistakes of any kind, even though we have never actually seen them."[6]

We are left to wonder about the value of perfect but nonexistent texts. This is at best a confused argument. It reasons that if we are to have implicit faith in the scriptures, they must be without error; yet it admits that no such scripture exists. Such a position is necessitated only by the errant dogma of sufficiency in the first place, and is without scriptural justification in the second. Obviously God does not share our Bible zealot's concern over inerrancy. For his purposes, it appears, it is enough that the scriptures be sufficiently plain that the honest in heart cannot misunderstand what is required of them, even though those seeking to make mischief can also find scriptural texts in which to clothe their folly.

Myth number four: *The Lord would not reveal something that we could not understand.* There is much within the canon of scripture that is deliberately ambiguous. "The things of God," said Joseph Smith "are of deep import; and time, and experience, and careful and ponderous and solemn thoughts can only find them out."[7] As treasures are rarely found on the surface, so an understanding of much that has been revealed and prophesied can be understood only by those who search the scriptures. In some measure the scriptures are as a sealed book, the various seals being destined to be broken, each in its turn, according to the timetable of the Lord. It is our privilege to see and understand some things in holy writ that were sealed to those of generations past, and it will yet be the privilege of future generations to see and understand in plainness that which we could not. As it is with canonized revelations, so it is with personal revelations. As we must grow up into an understanding of the scriptures, so we must grow up into an understanding of our patriarchal blessings.

It is neither required nor necessary that we understand all things at once. As one writer observed: "It would be a cold world in which no sun shone until the inhabitants thereof had arrived at a true chemical analysis of sunlight."[8] Thus it is with the light of revelation: we do not need to fully understand it in order to feel its warmth and be sustained by its life-giving power.

Myth number five: *The language of the revelations is exact.* The writers of the New Testament had little concern about preserving the exact language of Old Testament prophets as they quoted them. Scores of Old Testament texts are quoted in the New Testament with variations. As to our ancient texts, the Septuagint often deviates substantially from the Masoretic, leaving the impression that the emphasis was on concepts rather than on words. As scriptural texts are translated into the seemingly limitless number of tongues spoken among the kindred of this earth, exact wording becomes impossible. In any event, literal translations frequently fail to reach the true sense and meaning. It will be remembered that in quoting to Joseph Smith the Malachi passage relative to the return of Elijah, Moroni expressed it differently from the way it appears in the Old Testament and the Book of Mormon.[9] The fact that Moroni did so suggests that exact wording is not a matter of concern, and that scripture is subject to levels of translation. Teaching this principle, Brigham Young stated:

When God speaks to the people, he does it in a manner to suit their circumstances and capacities. He spoke to the children of Jacob through Moses, as a blind, stiff-necked people, and when Jesus and his Apostles came they talked with the Jews as a benighted, wicked, selfish people. They would not receive the Gospel, though presented to them by the Son of God in all its righteousness, beauty and glory. Should the Lord Almighty send an angel to re-write the Bible, it would in many places be very different from what it is now. And I will even venture to say that if the Book of Mormon were now to be re-written, in many instances it would materially differ from the present translation. According as people are willing to receive the things of God, so the heavens send forth their blessings. If the people are stiff-necked, the Lord can tell them but little.[10]

It is a misconception to suppose that the language used in the scriptures represents precise words used by the Lord.[11] Many passages of scripture, like the passage prophesying the return of Elijah, are subject to more than one correct translation. Though the things in the forepart of the book of Genesis are true, the book of Moses does to them what Moroni did to the Malachi prophecy, that is, it greatly expands them. So we have two differing translations of Genesis and both are true. The Gospel of John is a good New Testament illustration of this principle. The King James Translation begins by stating, "In the beginning was the Word, and the Word was with God, and the Word was God." The announcement is wholly true as it stands, yet the Joseph Smith Translation begins with the declaration: "In the beginning was the gospel preached through the Son. And the gospel was the word, and the word was with the Son, and the Son was with God, and the Son was of God." Thus the truths of the second translation take us beyond that rendered in the first.

Summarizing this principle, Elder McConkie said: "There can be two translations of the same thing and both of them can be true. One of them is designed as a translation to present the gospel to people who have a limited understanding and the other is a translation for people who have grown in the things of the Spirit and are prepared and capable of receiving more."[12]

Truths Fundamental to the Spirit of Prophecy

Lehi testified that "the Spirit is the same, yesterday, today, and forever" (2 Nephi 2:4). That is to say, the spirit of revelation operates according to the same principles in all generations. To know and understand how that spirit functioned anciently is to know and understand how that spirit functions today. Thus we can identify the following as among the principles that are common to the spirit of prophecy:

Revelations can properly be interpolated. The Bible, noted Elder McConkie, *"is not complete in any instance* [nor is any other scriptural text, for that matter]. If Mormon could have just had the ancient records of Israel, and done to them what he did to the records of the Nephites, and given us an account of Israel's history by inspiration, and then if we could receive it in translation the way he gave it, the Old Testament would read just exactly the way the Book of Mormon reads. It would talk about atonement, faith and repentance, gifts of the Spirit, the fall of Adam, and so on, the same way that the Book of Mormon does. But the Old Testament hasn't come to us that way. It has come to us in a degenerated form, it has come to us with many plain and precious things, as the angel told Nephi, taken out of the original text. So we don't have the Bible the way it once was, not even with the Inspired Version corrections. They don't begin to do all that needs to be done to the Bible. There are a lot of places in the Bible where it is talking about the restoration of the gospel and the gathering of Israel, as for instance in the thirty-seventh chapter of Ezekiel or the twenty-ninth chapter of Isaiah, that I could take and rewrite and make them twice as long as they are and they would then conform to the doctrine that was being taught by Ezekiel or Isaiah in each instance, which is only preserved to us in a fragmentary form."[13]

Targumming is perfectly appropriate. The Targums were explanations of the Hebrew scriptures in Aramaic for the benefit of a people who no longer understood their mother tongue. To targum is simply to paraphrase in such a manner as to catch the sense and feel of what is intended without a particular concern for precise language. After the Jews returned from their Babylonian captivity, Ezra assembled them to hear the reading of the Law. The instance is cited as the first occasion (though it surely could not have been) in which the scriptures were targummed. Ezra and his priests, we are told, "read in the book in the law of God distinctly, and gave the sense, and caused them to understand the reading" (Nehemiah 8:8). In like manner the Lord, having given Moses the Law on Sinai, commanded him to write it, saying: "Write thou these words: for after the *tenor of these words* I have made a covenant with thee and with Israel" (Exodus 34:27, italics added).

The spirit of prophecy, not past scripture, directs the Church. Mankind has not always had a Bible. Indeed; no one in Bible times had the Bible as we know it today. The apostasy in the meridian of time was complete long before the books we know as the New Testament were even codified in book form.[14] Plainly, in what we call "biblical times" there was no Bible. As one scholar notes: "Biblical faith, the faith of the men of the Bible, was not in its own nature a scriptural religion. Faith and religion, within the Bible, were not faith and religion defined and determined by a Bible."[15] It is, in fact, nonbiblical to claim a biblical religion! To build a religion upon the Bible is to build upon a foundation not known to the peoples of the Bible. "Completed scripture was something that was not there until a long time after the central events, after the time—if we may so call it—of biblical revelation was past: for the New Testament, one or two generations, perhaps more, and for the Old Testament, or almost all of it, some centuries."[16]

It was the spirit of prophecy and revelation that directed the affairs of the faithful in Bible times, not an established scriptural canon. "The prophets, from Elijah and Elisha in the ninth century, through Amos, Hosea, Isaiah, and Micah in the eighth, and down to those like Zechariah, Haggai, and Malachi after the return from exile, spoke of God, and one of their key phrases was 'Thus says the Lord'; but they did not speak on the basis of an already existing scripture, they did not mention any such scripture, and there is no evidence that such material, conceived as 'scripture', played a significant part in their minds. Rather, their speech was spontaneous, they spoke as God himself directly gave them speech. Old Testament man related to God much more through holy persons and institutions, and through a sort of direct personal and verbal communication with God, and little or not at all through pre-existing written and authoritative holy books."[17]

Scriptural records appear to have played a more important role in the New World than they did among the Old Testament peoples. Nonetheless the Book of Mormon makes it abundantly clear that the constitution of the Church among the Nephites was not a fixed canon but the spirit of prophecy and revelation as it rested on living prophets. Neither in the New World or the Old do we find the faithful being governed by revelations given to others. The Lord's people on both continents assumed the responsibility to receive revelation for their own circumstance. It was only when Israel was in a state of apostasy, for instance during the ministry of Christ, that the Jewish nation was governed by scripture rather than by living oracles. With the Church organized by Christ, the Old Testament, though of undisputed authority, was not viewed as a communicator of salvation. The testimony that the Christian missionary was charged to take to all the world was not that the Old Testament contained the word of God, and certainly it did, but rather that Christ had suffered, died, and risen again, and that salvation was in him and him only. This testimony was wholly supported by the Old Testament, and the Old Testament was an invaluable aid in teaching it, yet it was not the source of that testimony. Only the witness of the spirit of prophecy was accepted as a viable source for such teachings.

History clearly establishes the pattern—the Church is not to be governed by scriptural texts, as valuable as they may be. The constitution of the Church must be, as it has always been among those from whom our scriptures have come, the spirit of prophecy as it has rested upon those whom the Lord has called to lead his people. Though the revelations given to others are an invaluable help, they do not and cannot supplant the responsibility for personal communication with God. A second-hand religion is without the power of salvation.

A thing can be inspired and still be imperfect. It is a tenet of faith among Latter-day Saints that the Constitution of the United States is an inspired document. It is not, however, a tenet of our faith that the Constitution is without imperfections. Indeed, the inspiration of the Constitution allows for its own alteration. So it is with the revelations governing the kingdom of God—they need not be perfect to have claim upon a divine origin. Though we are offspring of God, that does not require that we profess perfection, though the capacity to become such rests within us. As with people, so with the written word: scripture need not profess perfection in order to claim a divine origin.

Surely if the scriptures are inerrant and infallible, as so many in our day declare them to be, one might ask, "why don't they say so?" Such an "oversight" on the Lord's part hardly sustains the idea of scriptural perfection. Further, if the scriptures are without fault of any sort we are left to wonder whether it would take faith to believe in them? And if it did not take faith to believe in them, how could they accomplish their object of fostering faith?

Functions of the Spirit of Prophecy

It is axiomatic that all God does is purposeful, appropriate, and necessary, and that his ultimate intent in all things is the exaltation of his children (see Moses 1:39). It follows that the heavens are always open to the obedient and honest truth-seeker. To such, God has promised he will give liberally without reproof. Typically, such divine help comes in the form of exhortation, warning, comfort, and edification. Let us briefly consider each.

To exhort. In the fullest sense, principles of true religion are found not in their proclamation but in their application. The praise of truth is not a substitute for the application of truth. Religion exists only where religion is practiced. When asked what is their faith, many modern Christians simply point to the Bible. That is similar to asking an athlete to show his muscles and his pointing to some dumb-bells. James admonishes us to be "doers of the word, and not hearers only," for such, he said, deceive themselves (James 1:22). It naturally follows that the Spirit which comes from the Lord is one of exhortation. By its very nature such a spirit will be found appealing and will urge all who listen to follow it to greater works of righteousness.

To warn. Frequently the spirit of prophecy comes as a voice of warning. Warnings and admonitions are common to both institutional and personal revelation. The Lord's preface to the Doctrine and Covenants is known to us as "the voice of warning" (D&C 1:4). In it the Lord commands that the restored gospel be proclaimed throughout the world, for only in that gospel can protection be found from the calamities that are to come upon the inhabitants of the earth (D&C 1:17–18). Similarly, by way of illustration, warnings and admonitions are common to personal or patriarchal blessings. As much of that which is communicated by wise parents to their children comes in the form of warning and admonition, so it is with the instruction that we receive from our Eternal Father.

To comfort. The manifestations of heaven are so frequently associated with feelings of love, solace, and assurance, all of which bring comfort to the souls of men, that both Christ and the Holy Ghost are known by the title *Comforter.* As used in the New Testament the words translated "comfort" are *parakaleo* (verb) and *paraklesis* (noun). The word literally means "called to one's side," having as its context the rendering of help. In particular *parakletos* means a helper or advocate in court who would speak on behalf of the accused. Christ, who is the advocate of the repentant sinner in the Father's court, naturally bears the title *parakletos*. In the general sense as used in the scriptures the reference is to "a helper, succorer, aider, or assistant."[18] Thus the role of the Holy Ghost is to lead into a deeper knowledge of gospel truths all who enjoy his companionship, and give them divine strength to accomplish the Lord's work and to come off victorious regardless of the trials they may face.

To edify. By revelation we are told "that which doth not edify is not of God, and is darkness" (D&C 50:23). Conversely we could say "that which edifies is of God, and is light." Anciently the verb "to edify" meant to build sacred edifices such as temples or chapels. Through the years the word *edify* has come to describe the process of improving character or building spirituality. All that is of God edifies—that is, it lifts, builds, and improves; conversely, to edify is to eschew that which demeans, belittles, or excuses. To edify is to make the body and soul of man a holy tabernacle, a temple to God. If a doctrine does not offer the opportunity to reach, to build, or to improve, it is not of God.

Requisites to the Spirit of Prophecy

There are requisites to the spirit of prophecy and revelation as there are to all other spirits. These requisites embrace the following:

Righteousness. Be it remembered that when the angel of the Lord visited Cornelius he said, "Thine alms are come up for a memorial before God" (Acts 10:4). Thus consideration and charity for others opened the heavens to Cornelius and qualified him to entertain a heavenly messenger. Similarly, when an angel of the Lord visited King Benjamin, the angel told him: "The Lord hath heard thy prayers, and hath judged of thy righteousness" (Mosiah 3:4). The scriptural declaration of the principle is "that the powers of heaven cannot be controlled nor handled only upon the principles of righteousness" (D&C 121:36).

Joseph Smith taught that "the gift of the Holy Ghost by the laying on of hands, cannot be received through the medium of any other principle than the principle of righteousness."[19] Where there is no righteousness the Spirit withdraws. The principle is taught in the Old Testament ritual of washing and anointing. The washing, which represented a cleansing of the soul, always preceded the anointing, which represented the outpouring of the Spirit.

Heed and Diligence. "It is given unto many to know the mysteries of God," Alma declared. "Nevertheless they are laid under a strict command that they shall not impart only according to the portion of his word which he doth grant unto the children of men, according to the heed and diligence which they give unto him. And therefore, he that will harden his heart, the same receiveth the lesser portion of the word; and he that will not harden his heart, to him is given the greater portion of the word, until it is given unto him to know the mysteries of God until he know them in full." (Alma 12:9–10.)

Alma's doctrine is that puny preparation precedes puny revelations. Joseph Smith said: "I could explain a hundred fold more than I ever have of the glories of the kingdoms manifested to me in the vision, were I permitted, and were the people prepared to receive them. The Lord deals with this people as a tender parent with a child, communicating light and intelligence and the knowledge of his ways as they can bear it."[20] The scriptural promise is that those who "hunger and thirst after righteousness" shall be "filled with the Holy Ghost" (3 Nephi 12:6). No such promise is given to those satisfied to nibble at the gospel or who fill themselves with spiritual junk food.

Scriptural Study. Scripture is simply the spirit of prophecy in its recorded form. Holy writ is our textbook in how the spirit of prophecy functions. Through the study of the standard works we can become familiar with the Spirit of truth and invite and entice that Spirit into our own lives. "Many, if not most, of the founding revelations of our dispensation were born of scriptural study. It was the text in James that led Joseph Smith to what we know as the Sacred Grove and his divine appointment with the Father and the Son. It was the pondering of Book of Mormon passages about baptism that led Joseph Smith and Oliver Cowdery to the banks of the Susquehanna River, where their imploring of the heavens was answered by John the Baptist and the restoration of the Aaronic Priesthood. It was concern over a text in the Gospel of John (D&C 76:15) that resulted in our receiving the greatest revelation of our and perhaps of any dispensation—the revelation on the degrees of glory. 'I sat in my room pondering over the scriptures,' wrote Joseph F. Smith, as he described the circumstances that called forth the great revelation on the redemption of the dead. (D&C 138:1-2, 11.) Again and again the principle has proven itself: nothing is more effective in prompting the spirit of revelation than the study of revelation."[21] Elder Bruce R. McConkie said, "Those who study, ponder, and pray about the scriptures, seeking to understand their deep and hidden meanings, receive from time to time great outpourings of light and knowledge from the Holy Spirit."[22]

A Reverent Spirit. The things of God are not to be trifled with, nor are we to ask for that which we ought not (D&C 6:12; 8:10). "Remember," Joseph Smith was warned, "that that which cometh from above is sacred, and must be spoken with care, and by constraint of the Spirit" (D&C 63:64). Even to the Saints the knowledge of heaven is as a "hidden treasure." Heaven's treasures are given for the benefit of those who love God and keep all his commandments, and those "that seeketh so to do; that all may be benefited that seek or that ask" of God, "that ask and not for a sign that they may consume it upon their lusts" (D&C 46:9). "Whatsoever ye ask the Father in my name," the Savior promised, "it shall be given unto you, *that is expedient for you;* and if ye ask anything that is not expedient for you, it shall turn unto your condemnation" (D&C 88:64-65, italics added).

A Listening Ear. "Faith comes by hearing the word of God through the testimony of the servants of God," Joseph Smith taught, and added the assurance that "that testimony is always attended by the Spirit of prophecy and revelation."[23] To be instructed in the principles of the kingdom is at the same time to be inspired by those principles because their spirit is one of inspiration. Eternal principles cannot be learned independent of the spirit of prophecy and revelation. That is their source and must, therefore, be the source from which an understanding of them comes.

A Conducive Place. On the heels of the restoration of the priesthood came the charge to build a temple "that the Son of Man might have a place to manifest himself to his people" (D&C 109:5). As Adam walked with God in Eden, so Abraham saw him at Haran and Moriah, Jacob at Peniel, Moses at Sinai. Enoch had his Mount Simeon, the brother of Jared Mount Shelem, and Christ, Peter, James, and John the Mount of Transfiguration. Such places have been consecrated of the Lord for their sacred and holy purposes. For our day "the mountain of the Lord's house" is the temple. There we too are entitled to enjoy those experiences common to the spiritually inclined of ages past. Upon such sacred ground the Lord has promised the outpouring of his Spirit (D&C 109:12–13).

Rituals or Covenants. The spirit of prophecy and revelation is commonly associated with the making of covenants. Recounting the events that attended the restoration of the Aaronic Priesthood and the ordinance of baptism, Joseph Smith wrote: "No sooner had I baptized Oliver Cowdery, than the Holy Ghost fell upon him, and he stood up and prophesied many things which should shortly come to pass. And again, so soon as I had been baptized by him, I also had the spirit of prophecy, when, standing up, I prophesied concerning the rise of this Church, and many other things connected with the Church, and this generation of the children of men. We were filled with the Holy Ghost, and rejoiced in the God of our salvation." (Joseph Smith—History 1:73.)

With the restoration of the higher or Melchizedek Priesthood came "the key of the knowledge of God," and the announcement that in the ordinances of the priesthood "the power of godliness is manifest," including the invitation to see him face to face (D&C 84:19–22). "The power and authority of the higher, or Melchizedek Priesthood is to hold the keys of all the spiritual blessings of the church—to have the privilege of receiving the mysteries of the kingdom of heaven, to have the heavens opened unto them, to commune with the general assembly and church of the Firstborn, and to enjoy the communion and presence of God the Father, and Jesus the mediator of the new covenant" (D&C 107:18–19).

Conclusions

1. The issue in translation is not so much getting back to the original language as it is in getting back to the original spirit. It was the "gift and power of God," not a mastery of ancient tongues, that enabled Joseph Smith to translate the Book of Mormon. The restoration of the authority by which the gift of the Holy Ghost is given is more important in the process of translation than the restoration of ancient texts. Indeed, in the instance of Doctrine and Covenants section 7 and the Joseph Smith Translation no text was necessary. The Bible, notwithstanding the scholarship and erudition that has gone into its translation, remains a sealed book even to its translators. True understanding comes only as the Spirit comes. Describing the experience of having the Holy Ghost fall upon himself and Oliver Cowdery, Joseph Smith wrote: "Our minds being now enlightened, we began to have the scriptures laid open to our understandings, and the true meaning and intention of their more mysterious passages revealed unto us in a manner which we never could attain to previously, nor ever before had thought of" (Joseph Smith—History 1:74).

Though the words that Joseph and Oliver read remained

the same, the meaning they conveyed was now appreciably different. Now if Joseph or Oliver were to translate these passages in which "the true meaning and intention" had been revealed to them—and this is precisely what the Prophet was doing in the Joseph Smith Translation—their obligation in translation would be to convey the deeper or more complete meaning rather than simply to translate words. Again, the key to translation is gospel understanding, not language mastery. Thus if Mormon were to have translated the texts of the Old Testament it would read like the Book of Mormon. It would contain references to baptism, Christ, resurrection, spiritual gifts, the Holy Ghost, and so forth, just as the Joseph Smith Translation does.

This is not a matter of a prophet reading his own culture into ancient texts, as some have supposed. It is a recognition of the verity that the gospel is everlastingly the same, and that it is not, as many suppose, a result of an evolutionary process. The whole concept of the restoration of the gospel is that we have been given anew what the ancients had. We profess no priesthood, keys, power, or authority that we did not receive from them. They have been our tutors, their priesthood is our priesthood, their doctrines our doctrines, their rituals our rituals. Surely it is foolish to suppose that in our day we have a system of salvation that differs from or is superior to theirs.

2. As to the words in which revelations are given, it ought to be noted that words are but servants, the message is their master. Whether large or small, graceful or awkward, colorful or colorless, they have value only to the extent that they convey understanding with the sense and feeling intended. It is the message that is important, not the messenger. It is the truths within the Book of Mormon that are important, not the fact that Moroni brought it to us rather than Mormon or Nephi. Many heard the voice of Christ in the meridian day; few heard the message. Many profess great reverence for the Bible; few understand its purpose and meaning.

3. A primary purpose of all revelation is to attest that God always has spoken and always will speak to those who have ears to hear and eyes to see. The right to the spirit of prophecy and revelation is fundamental to citizenry in God's earthly kingdom. As to the mode of its coming, we would but say it comes "at sundry times and in divers manners." The scriptural formula for receiving it is simply to study, pray, and obey. One cannot grovel and enjoy the Spirit of the Lord. Conversely, one cannot live as he or she ought and not enjoy that Spirit.

Notes

1. *Teachings*, p. 149.
2. For a listing and description of these translations, see Kubo and Specht, *So Many Versions?*
3. Isaiah's reference to leviathan (Isaiah 27:1) appears to be figurative. Job also refers to behemoth (Job 40:15–24), which is described in apocryphal and pseudepigraphal sources as leviathan's male counterpart though living in marshes rather than the sea (2 Baruch 29:4; 2 Esdras 6:49, 52).
4. Buttric, *The Interpreter's Bible*, 5:261–64.
5. Buttric, *The Interpreter's Bible*, 6:1142.
6. Archer, *Encyclopedia of Bible Difficulties*, p. 29.
7. *Teachings*, p. 137.
8. Hatch, *The Influence of Greek Ideas on Christianity*, p. 333.
9. Because the passage is quoted in the Book of Mormon (3 Nephi 25:5–6) as it appears in the Old Testament (Malachi 4:5–6), we assume the Old Testament rendering to be correct, notwithstanding that Moroni quoted it quite differently to Joseph Smith (D&C 2; Joseph Smith—History 1:36–39).
10. *Journal of Discourses*, 9:311.
11. Bruce R. McConkie, from an unpublished talk given to prospective Book of Mormon teachers at Brigham Young University, June 13, 1984. A copy of the talk, which was approved by him, is in the possession of the author.
12. Bruce R. McConkie, unpublished talk, June 13, 1984.
13. Bruce R. McConkie, unpublished talk, June 13, 1984.

14. The earliest known reference to the New Testament as we have it is A.D. 367 (Schaff and Wace, *Nicene and Post-Nicene Fathers of the Christian Church*, 4:551–52.)

15. Barr, *Holy Scripture: Canon, Authority, Criticism*, pp. 1–2.

16. Barr, *Holy Scripture*, p. 3.

17. Barr, *Holy Scripture*, p. 5.

18. Thayer, *The New Thayer's Greek-English Lexicon of the New Testament*, p. 483; see also Kittel and Friedrich, *Theological Dictionary of the New Testament*, pp. 782–84.

19. *Teachings*, p. 148.

20. *History of the Church*, 5:402.

21. Joseph Fielding McConkie, *The Spirit of Revelation*, p. 34.

22. Joseph Fielding McConkie, *The Spirit of Revelation*, p. 34.

23. *Teachings*, p. 148.

8

Scriptures Foreknown

> *My works are without end, and also my words, for they never cease.*
> —Moses 1:4
>
> *Wherefore murmur ye, because that ye shall receive more of my word?*
> —2 Nephi 29:8

From the days of Adam the prophets of the Lord have spoken longingly of a great day of restoration that will usher in the millennial kingdom (Acts 3:21; D&C 86:10). Their prophecies include the promise that the tribes of Israel will again inherit their ancient promised lands, that the covenant people will return to their faith in the God of Abraham, Isaac, and Jacob, and that the priesthood with all its keys, powers, and majesties will be restored (Isaiah 52:1–2; D&C 113:7–10). Often overlooked in this epic story of restoration are the promises relative to the restoration of scriptural texts. Since Israel's restoration is first and foremost to God—the God of their fathers and the covenant of salvation he made with them—one of the most significant parts of this story centers in the restoration and gathering of long-lost books of scripture. Let us review these promises.

Lost Scripture

Only a small portion of the prophecies and revelations recorded in times past are now available to us. The library of lost scripture contains many volumes that are destined to unite their testimony with the scriptural remnants we now have. This restoration of holy writ will involve more than just "plain and precious parts" that have been taken from or lost to extant records. Volumes of books, each in their proper time, will be brought forth, some of which may far exceed in depth and breadth all that we presently have. Things from the days of Adam (Moses 6:5) to "the account of the words spoken by the angelic ministrants who restored the Melchizedek Priesthood" in our own dispensation are yet to be restored.[1]

As righteous souls from the days of Adam and Eve to Zacharias and Elisabeth anxiously anticipated the birth of Christ, and as all the holy prophets have revelled in the promise of a time when all things would be restored, so we, in eager expectancy, look to a future day when the knowledge of the noble and great ones of ages past will be restored to us. We have been assured that in that day when we have proven our faith, made ourselves clean, and become a people sanctified before the Lord, sealed books will be opened and all things from the beginning will be made known. Let us review these promises of a scriptural gathering—this restoration of the knowledge and faith of the ancients.

Book of Mormon Promises of a Scriptural Gathering

Sealed Portion of the Book of Mormon

It is common knowledge among Latter-day Saints that the Lord allowed Joseph Smith to translate only a portion of the plates from which the Book of Mormon came. "He has translated the book," the Lord said, "even that part which I have commanded him, and as your Lord and your God liveth it is true" (D&C 17:6). That Joseph Smith would be allowed to translate only a portion of the record was announced by Nephi. Describing the sealed portion of the Book of Mormon, Nephi wrote:

> In the book shall be a revelation from God, from the beginning of the world to the ending thereof.
> Wherefore, because of the things which are sealed up, the things which are sealed shall not be delivered

in the day of the wickedness and abominations of the people. Wherefore the book shall be kept from them.
. . .
For the book shall be sealed by the power of God, and the revelation which was sealed shall be kept in the book until the own due time of the Lord, that they may come forth; for behold, they reveal all things from the foundation of the world unto the end thereof.

And the day cometh that the words of the book which were sealed shall be read upon the house tops; and they shall be read by the power of Christ; and all things shall be revealed unto the children of men which ever have been among the children of men, and which ever will be even unto the end of the earth. (2 Nephi 27:7–8, 10–11.)

We look to the sealed part of the Book of Mormon to give us an "account of life in preexistence; of the creation of all things; of the fall and the Atonement, and the Second Coming; of temple ordinances in their fullness; of the ministry and mission of translated beings; of life in the spirit world, in both paradise and hell; of the kingdoms of glory to be inhabited by resurrected beings, and many such like things," wrote Elder Bruce R. McConkie.[2]

Mormon said he would have written more but "the Lord forbade it." However, he explained, those who accept in faith that which he did write have the promise of receiving "greater things," while those who reject them will have all such things "withheld from them, unto their condemnation." (3 Nephi 26:6–11.) Moroni added that "never" had "greater things" been manifest than those contained in the sealed portion of the Book of Mormon, and that they are not to go forth until men "repent of their iniquity, and become clean before the Lord." They will only come forth in a day of faith, a day when men have sanctified and prepared themselves for the revelation of all things. (See Ether 4:4–7.)

Nephite and Jaredite Records to Come Forth

The Book of Mormon is merely an abridgment of records kept by the ancient inhabitants of the American continent.

The abridgers were Mormon and his son Moroni. Mormon was the compiler and editor of everything from the Words of Mormon to the end of 4 Nephi. He then added seven chapters of a book which bears his name. Moroni completed his father's book (chapters 8 and 9), abridged the book of Ether, and authored a ten-chapter book in his own name (chapters 7–9 of which comprise a speech and writings of his father's), which concludes the Book of Mormon. Both men lamented that they were able to include but "a hundredth part" of what they desired. Mormon said this in reference to what Christ taught the Nephites during his ministry among them (3 Nephi 26:6–7), Moroni in reference to his abridgment of the twenty-four plates of gold which are the source from which the book of Ether has come (Ether 15:33).

We anticipate a future day when not only will we be blessed with all that was originally included on the gold plates from which the Book of Mormon came, but also its original source materials—i.e., the brass plates, the plates of Nephi, and the entirety of what was contained on the twenty-four plates of gold, or what might be called the plates of Ether. Mormon tells us that Christ "did expound all things even from the beginning until the time that he should come in his glory—yea, even all things which should come upon the face of the earth, even until the elements should melt with fervent heat, and the earth should be wrapt together as a scroll, and the heavens and the earth should pass away" (3 Nephi 26:3).

Secreted within the Hill Cumorah, we are told, is a library of sacred records. According to President Brigham Young: "Oliver Cowdery went with the Prophet Joseph when he deposited these plates. Joseph did not translate all of the plates; there was a portion of them sealed, which you can learn from the Book of Doctrine and Covenants. When Joseph got the plates, the angel instructed him to carry them back to the hill Cumorah, which he did. Oliver says that when Joseph and Oliver went there, the hill opened, and they walked into a cave, in which there was a large and spacious room. He says he did not think, at the time, whether they had the light of the sun or artificial light; but that it was just as light as day. They laid the plates on a table; it was a large table that stood in the room. Under this table there was a pile of plates as much as two feet high, and there were altogether in this room more plates than probably many wagon loads; they were piled up in the corners and along the walls. The first time they went there the sword of Laban hung upon the wall; but when they went again it had been taken down and laid upon the table across the gold plates; it was unsheathed, and on it was written these words: 'This sword will never be sheathed again until the kingdoms of this world become the kingdom of our God and his Christ.' "[3]

David Whitmer, who, along with Oliver Cowdery, was also a special witness of the Book of Mormon, said: "Joseph, Oliver, and myself were together when I saw them [the gold plates]. We not only saw the plates of the Book of Mormon, but also the brass plates, the plates of the Book of Ether . . . and many other plates . . . there appeared, as it were, a table with many records, or plates, upon it, besides the plates of the Book of Mormon, also the sword of Laban, the directors [Liahona], and the interpreters."[4]

The Brass Plates to Be Restored

While Lehi and his little company rested in the valley of Lemuel the patriarch was commanded to send his sons back to Jerusalem to obtain a scriptural record which had been engraved on plates of brass. This record contained things written by "all the holy prophets" from Adam to Jeremiah (see 1 Nephi 3:20; 5:13). The plates were in the possession of a powerful and unscrupulous man by the name of Laban, and it was only by divine intervention that Lehi's sons were able to obtain them. Such was the spirit of the brass plates that when Lehi read them he was filled with the spirit of revelation and prophesied that these "plates of brass [presumably meaning their content] should go forth unto all nations, kindreds, tongues, and people who were of his seed." Further, Lehi said that they would "never perish" or be "dimmed" by the passage of time. (1 Nephi 5:18–19.)

It appears that the prophecy of Lehi received repeated confirmation by the voice of Nephite prophets. More than five centuries later Alma the Younger said it had "been prophesied by our fathers, that [the plates of brass] should be kept and handed down from one generation to another, and be kept and preserved by the hand of the Lord until they should go forth unto every nation, kindred, tongue, and people, that they shall know of the mysteries contained thereon." Alma also affirmed that the plates would retain their brightness and added the prophesy that all the plates in the Nephite library of holy writ would, in like manner, retain their brightness. (Alma 37:4–5.)

A partial fulfillment of this prophecy can be found in the taking of the Book of Mormon to the nations of the earth. This is so simply because the Book of Mormon prophets quoted so freely from the brass plates. In the full and complete sense, however, it is evident that this record is to go forth as a companion witness to such records as the Bible and the Book of Mormon. The contents of the brass plates include a pure rendering of "the five books of Moses, which give an account of the creation of the world, and also of Adam and Eve, who were our first parents; and also a record of the Jews from the beginning, even down to the commencement of the reign of Zedekiah, king of Judah; and also the prophecies of the holy prophets, from the beginning, even down to the commencement of the reign of Zedekiah; and also many prophecies which have been spoken by the mouth of Jeremiah" (1 Nephi 5:11–13). In addition they contain a detailed genealogy that enabled Lehi to trace his ancestral line to Manasseh and through him to Joseph, Jacob, Isaac, and Abraham, with whom the Lord made eternal covenants relative to their posterity (1 Nephi 5:14; Alma 37:3).

When it comes forth, the testimony of the brass plates will constitute a pure version of the Old Testament from the story of the Creation to the point in time that the Book of Mormon record begins. In spirit and doctrine it will be one with the Nephite record. Like the Book of Mormon it will testify to the Jews that their forefathers taught and testified of

Christ, having a perfect knowledge of the saving principles of his gospel. It will attest that the doctrine of Christ was the doctrine of Abraham, Isaac, and Jacob. In fact, we are told that the brass plates constitute a more extensive scriptural record than the Bible (1 Nephi 13:23). Not only will it expose false traditions but it also will set at naught scholarly theories that suppose an evolving theology among Old Testament peoples. Along with the restoration of doctrines and covenants to the stick of Judah, the translation of the brass plates will also give us that sacred history in a plainness and simplicity that in many instances has been lost from the Bible.

Promise of Scriptures Once Possessed by the Lost Tribes

Through the pen of Nephi the Lord promised that in the last days "it shall come to pass that the Jews shall have the words of the Nephites, and the Nephites shall have the words of the Jews; and the Nephites and the Jews shall have the words of the lost tribes of Israel; and the lost tribes of Israel shall have the words of the Nephites and the Jews. And it shall come to pass that my people, which are of the house of Israel, shall be gathered home unto the lands of their possessions; and my word also shall be gathered in one." (2 Nephi 29:13–14.)

There are at least three things of particular interest in Nephi's prophecy. First, the announcement that we will yet receive scriptural records from the lost tribes, which affirms that, along with the testimony of Jesus, the repentant of the lost tribes also had prophets, priesthood, and the ordinances of salvation; second, that there is to be a great gathering of scriptural records in the last days; third, that the testimony of all nations is to run together into one great affirmation of Christ. It will be as if all nations and generations assembled to be instructed by one another.

A Restoration of Old Testament Books

We look to see the great scriptural gathering of the last days include appreciably more than refinements of various

Old Testament verses. Our anticipation is that we will enjoy an avalanche of restored texts. From revelations of the Restoration we conclude that the assembled records will include "the book of the generations of Adam" (Moses 6:8); the book of Enoch, which undoubtedly contains prophecies of all that will befall the children of men "unto the latest generation" (D&C 107:56); and the writings of such prophets as Zenock, Neum, Zenos, and Ezias, all of whom testified with great power about the coming Christ (1 Nephi 19:10; Helaman 8:19–20).

Discussion of the lost books of the Bible usually centers in references to books in the Bible that no longer exist yet were accorded scriptural status among the ancients. They consist of at least the following: book of the wars of the Lord (Numbers 21:14); book of Jasher (Joshua 10, 13; 2 Samuel 1:18); book of the acts of Solomon (1 Kings 11:41); book of Samuel the seer (1 Chronicles 29:29); book of Gad the seer (1 Chronicles 29:29); book of Nathan the prophet (1 Chronicles 29:29; 2 Chronicles 9:29); book of Shemaiah (2 Chronicles 12:15); and acts of Uzziah, written by Isaiah (2 Chronicles 26:22).

Though we are without specific references or recorded promises, it seems reasonable to suppose that we will yet have writings from the likes of Seth, Enos, Cainan, Mahalaleel, Jared, Methusaleh, and Noah, all of whom prophesied before the Flood. That scripture was written by such as Shem, Melchizedek, Esaias[5], Jeremy, Elihu, Caleb, and Jethro also seems probable (D&C 84:7–13). The scroll from which our present book of Abraham came also had with it writings of Joseph of Egypt[6], of whom Nephi said: "He truly prophesied concerning all his seed. And the prophecies which he wrote, there are not many greater. And he prophesied concerning us, and our future generations." (2 Nephi 4:2.)

It ought also be observed that New Testament writers quoted books they considered canonical which are not included in the Old Testament as we have it today. In his epistle, Jude quotes two Old World sources as scripture that are not presently in the Old Testament. The first appears to be a pseudepigraphic work known as the Assumption of Moses[7]; the second, Jude attributed to Enoch (Jude 1:9, 14–15). The library of apocryphal and pseudepigraphic works presently includes three Enoch manuscripts. Scholars believe the first of these to be the work cited by Jude, and that it influenced the books of Matthew, Luke, John, Acts, Romans, 1 and 2 Corinthians, Ephesians, Colossians, 1 and 2 Thessalonians, 1 Timothy, Hebrews, and 1 John.[8] Given that we anticipate an eventual restoration of Enoch's writings, and that the above manuscripts do not contain the material we have been assured that Enoch recorded,[9] it is doubtful that either book presently exists as it did when Jude apparently quoted from it.

New Testament Texts Now Lost

When Joseph Smith and Oliver Cowdery disagreed on the matter of whether John the Revelator "tarried on earth or died," they inquired of the Lord through the Urim and Thummim and had contents of a parchment written and hidden up by John manifest to them (see D&C 7). In another revelation Joseph Smith was told that Peter, James, and John were shown the transfiguration of the earth during their experience on the Mount and that the time would yet come when we would be given an account of what was shown to them (see D&C 63:20–21). Doctrine and Covenants 93 quotes an extract from a record written by John the Baptist, with the promise that when we are sufficiently faithful it will be revealed to us. It is from these verses that we learn that Christ did not receive a fulness of his Father at first, but advanced from grace to grace until he received that fulness. (D&C 93:6–18.) In the commencement of his Gospel, Luke observed that "many" had likewise written of the same things as he was recording (see Luke 1:1). How many recorded these marvelous events we have no way of knowing, but one authority indicates that "originally there were at least eighty!"[10] We know that one of Paul's epistles of instruction to the Corinthians is lost to us (see 1 Corinthians 5:9). Though many pious frauds have been found in recent years, occasionally something is discovered that has the clear ring of truth. A leaf of a parchment book found in Middle Egypt in 1905 is one such example. It reads as follows:

> And he [Christ] took the disciples with him into the place of purification itself and walked about in the Temple court. And a Pharisaic chief priest, Levi by name, fell in with them and said to the Saviour: Who gave thee leave to tread this place of purification and to look upon these holy utensils without having bathed thyself and even without thy disciples having washed their feet? On the contrary, being defiled, thou hast trodden the Temple court, this clean place, although no one who has not first bathed himself or changed his clothes may tread it and venture to view these holy utensils! Forthwith the Saviour stood still with his disciples and answered: How stands it then with thee, thou art forsooth also here in the Temple court. Art thou then clean? He said to him: I am clean. For I have bathed myself in the pool of David and have gone down by the one stair and come up by the other and have put on white and clean clothes, and only then have I come hither and have viewed these holy utensils. Then said the Saviour to him: Woe unto you blind that see not! Thou hast bathed thyself in water that is poured out, in which dogs and swine lie night and day and thou hast washed thyself and has chafed thine outer skin, which prostitutes also and flute girls anoint, bathe, chafe and rouge, in order to arouse desire in men, but within they are full of scorpions and of badness of every kind. But I and my disciples, of whom thou sayest that we have not immersed ourselves, have been immersed in living water which comes down from [heaven].[11]

The Doctrinal Restoration

"In the dispensation of the fulness of times," the Apostle Paul declared, God shall "gather together in one all things in Christ, both which are in heaven, and which are on earth; even in him" (Ephesians 1:10). All things—things both temporal and spiritual—are to be restored to their pure and pristine state. Indeed, "the earth shall be like as it was in the days before it was divided," "yea, every valley shall be filled, and every mountain and hill shall be brought low," and the earth shall receive again its "paradisiacal glory" (D&C 133:24; JST, Luke 3:10; Articles of Faith 1:10). The ancients looked to this time of restitution with longing anticipation. The chief question asked by the Apostles of the resurrected Lord was: "Wilt thou at this time restore again the kingdom to Israel?" The gospel and its saving ordinances had been given to them. Now they desired to know when they as a nation would enjoy again the glory that Israel had known in the days of David. To their question, Christ simply responded, "It is not for you to know." (Acts 1:6–7.)

Latter-day Saints have been conditioned to think of this promised restitution of all things in terms of the restoration of the priesthood and the Church. Such a view is seriously incomplete. The remnants of Israel are to be gathered from the ends of the earth, and the glories of the ancient kingdom restored. Yet even the restoration of priesthood and its majesties is of no moment if the truths of salvation or the mysteries of heaven are not also restored. Nothing would be accomplished by returning Israel to her ancient lands in her ancient state of spiritual corruption and rebellion. It is to the knowledge of God, the saving principles of the gospel, that Israel must first return. The gathering must be first spiritual and then temporal, as the Book of Mormon so eloquently and repetitiously attests.[12] Israel must return in faith, and faith cannot be exercised in fables and falsehoods.

"Faith comes," Joseph Smith taught, "by hearing the word of God."[13] Indeed, the revelations of God are and have been the sure foundation for the exercise of faith among the Saints in all ages. Thus if the Latter-day Saints are to be on the same grounds as the former-day Saints they must have the same knowledge of the character and attributes of God as that possessed by those ancients.[14] This is simply a manifestation of the eternal verity that all things produce after their own kind. Faith produces faith, knowledge produces knowledge, and the spirit of revelation produces additional revelation. Thus when men lose their faith they "run into strifes, contentions, darkness, and difficulties," but "when faith comes it brings its train of attendants with it—apostles, prophets, evangelists, pastors, teachers, gifts, wisdom, knowledge, miracles, healings, tongues, interpretation of tongues, etc.," taught Joseph Smith. "All these appear when faith appears on the earth, and disappear when it disappears from the earth; for these are the effects of faith, and always have attended, and always will, attend it. For where faith is, there will the knowledge of God be also, with all things which pertain thereto—revelations, visions, and dreams, as well as every necessary thing, in order that the possessors of faith may be perfected, and obtain salvation."[15]

As nothing would be accomplished by restoring Israel to her ancient covenant lands unless she first returned to the faith and covenants of her fathers, so nothing could be accomplished by the restoration of the priesthood without restoring the gospel that priesthood is to administer (see D&C 84:19). It is not without significance that Joseph Smith was well into the translation of the Book of Mormon before the Aaronic Priesthood was restored, and that all that he did on the Joseph Smith Translation was completed before the first temple was built or Moses, Elias, Elijah and others returned with their keys. If we are to have faith and power of the ancients we must also have the knowledge of the ancients; thus the necessity of our possessing the revelations they possessed. The doctrinal restoration must precede the restoration of all other things.

Conclusion

The greatest event of the promised restitution of all things will not be the building of a temple in the Jerusalem of the Old World or the building of a temple in Jackson County,

Missouri. It will not be the uniting of all land mass in one, nor will it be the purging of the earth with fire. It is and will be the doctrinal restoration, the obtaining of the mind and will of God, the manifestation of that path which all must tread if they would again return to the divine presence. God is not honored by ignorance nor worshipped in error. Revealed truth is the foundation of all righteousness and faith, and thus we have the promise that all truths once spoken by God's anointed spokesmen are to be had again among us.

Notes

1. Bruce R. McConkie, *Mormon Doctrine*, p. 453.
2. McConkie and Millet, *Doctrinal Commentary on the Book of Mormon*, 1:316.
3. *Journal of Discourses*, 19:38.
4. Jenson, *Historical Record*, 6:208.
5. Esaias, who is spoken of in Doctrine and Covenants 76:100 and 84:13, is not to be confused with Isaiah, who is also spoken of in the Doctrine and Covenants 76 reference. It has been suggested that he may be one and the same with Ezias named in Helaman 8:20.
6. *History of the Church*, 2:236.
7. Butterworth, *Origen on First Principles*, p. 211.
8. Charlesworth, *The Old Testament Pseudepigrapha*, 1:10.
9. Enoch recorded the events of the conference held at Adam-ondi-Ahman and the things prophesied by Adam relative to his posterity to the end of time (D&C 107:56–57). The Enoch manuscripts presently available contain material suggesting some authenticity, but fall far short of the above description.
10. Barthel, *What The Bible Really Says*, p. 16.
11. Hennecke, *New Testament Apocrypha*, 1:92–93.
12. See for instance, 1 Nephi chapters 15 and 19; 2 Nephi chapters 6, 10, 25, 29, 30, and 33; 3 Nephi chapters 20 through 22; and Ether 13. Book of Mormon prophets are emphatic that Israel was scattered for rejecting Christ and are to be physically gathered only after they have once again accepted him. The creation of the modern state of Israel does not fulfill the prophecies about the

gathering of Israel as given in either the Bible or the Book of Mormon, though it could be thought of as the Reformation was to the Restoration. See Bruce R. McConkie, *A New Witness for the Articles of Faith*, pp. 510–619; also *The Millennial Messiah*, pp. 193–203, 319–29.

13. *Teachings*, p. 148.
14. Smith, *Lectures on Faith*, 3:25–26.
15. Smith, *Lectures on Faith*, 7:20.

9

The Discerning of Prophecy

> *The wisdom that is from above is first pure, then peaceable, gentle, and easy to be intreated, full of mercy and good fruits, without partiality, and without hypocrisy.*
> —James 3:17

The greatest truths are always opposed by the greatest heresies. The greater the outpouring of the spirit of truth, the greater the deluge of falsehoods that will follow. The legions of the adversary are seasoned warriors and are not about to retreat simply because the banners of truth have been unfolded. Ultimately truth will prevail, but it will not do so without opposition. Every truth of salvation will have its counterfeit, every principle of righteousness its impostor, every good cause its cortege of opportunists. False Christs, false prophets, false revelations, and false doctrines abound and "if possible, they shall deceive the very elect, who are the elect according to the covenant" (Joseph Smith—Matthew 1:22). Thus the warning: "Let every man beware lest he do that which is not in truth and righteousness before me" (D&C 50:9).

By what standards, then, do we discern between that which properly represents the God of heaven and devious or pious frauds? Such is the matter to which we now turn our attention, considering characteristics of both true religion and the spirit of revelation.

Characteristics of a True Religion

True religion must be miraculous in its nature. We have previously noted that all true religion is revealed religion. It is but a natural extension of this verity to say that all true religion must be premised on the supernatural or miraculous. Of necessity, true religion requires faith in its acceptance and faith in its observance. Without an omnipotent God, a God beyond the reasoning and powers of man, there can be no true religion.

True religion finds answers in the omnipotence of God. It is not earthbound, nor does it seek verification at the hands of mortal men. True religion will not seek answers in science or any other man-made discipline. Its principles and practices must profess to be rooted in heaven. No dogma conceived by mortal man has the power of immortality in it. Only that which comes from heaven can reside in heaven.

A sure knowledge of the doctrines of salvation must be within the grasp of all. If God were not a being in whom the attribute of justice was to be found in full and perfect measure, he would not be worthy of the worship of good and wholesome people. "Without the idea of the existence of the attribute justice in the Deity, men could not have confidence sufficient to place themselves under his guidance and direction," taught Joseph Smith. They would be filled, he said, "with fear and doubt lest the judge of all the earth would not do right, and thus fear or doubt, existing in the mind, would preclude the possibility of the exercise of faith in him for life and salvation."[1] From the knowledge that God is just, a knowledge born in the hearts of all men, it naturally follows that all who have or will have inhabited the earth will be granted the opportunity before the day of judgment to embrace the word of life unto salvation. For many, perhaps most who have lived upon the earth, that experience will come not in mortality but rather in the world of spirits, where they await the day when they will be called forth from the grave. (John 5:25–29; 1 Peter 3:18–20; 4:6; D&C 128.) The justice of God assures that, irrespective of the earthly prisons or chains of oppression with which they may have been bound, all will be free to accept and live the gospel or to reject its blessings if they so choose.

It is not enough that all mankind have equal opportunity to accept or reject the gospel. The justice of heaven also assures that all accountable people have innately within them the ability and capacity to know and recognize the truths of salvation. There is and can be, as we shall shortly show, but one plan or system by which men can be saved. There is no aristocracy where principles of truth are concerned. We do not have one system of salvation for the wealthy and learned and another for the impoverished and uncultured. All are born with the light of Christ; all who breathe the breath of life and are accountable before him have been endowed by their Maker with the ability and the capacity to distinguish between truth and error, light and darkness, good and evil. (D&C 84:45–48; 93:2; Moroni 7:16.) Were it not so, a just God could not proclaim an ultimate day of judgment. Were it not so, men could not in justice be held accountable for rejecting the principles of salvation or for warring against them.

Though all are aided by prophets and teachers, none in the justice of God are to be left dependent upon the experiences, learning, or understanding of others. No accountable soul is excused from the responsibility of working out his own salvation with fear and trembling (see Philippians 2:12). The ability to know that which God requires of us is within the grasp of all, as is the responsibility. All who can call God their Father, all who will eventually be called forth to a day of judgment, indeed all accountable souls, have been endowed with the capacity to understand and live the principles of salvation.

True religion is always viewed by the world as being intolerant. Mystics show sympathetic appreciation for all forms of religion, while prophets are fundamentally intolerant. Having entered the gate of falsehood himself, the mystic is naturally reluctant to close that gate to others. Commonly, those who vaunt their education and self-proclaimed enlightenment assume a condescending tolerance toward any and all religious views—with the frequent exception of the Restored

Church. True prophets, by contrast, have never shared this ecumenical spirit, being unable to make concessions to error.

Joshua's immortal charge to Israel was to put away the gods which their fathers had served in Egypt and serve the Lord. "Choose you this day," he said, "whom ye will serve; whether the gods which your fathers served that were on the other side of the flood, or the gods of the Amorites, in whose land ye dwell: but as for me and my house, we will serve the Lord." When his people responded that they would serve that God who had brought them out of Egypt, Joshua reminded them that Jehovah was a holy God and a jealous God who would reject them if they were to reject him. "If ye forsake the Lord, and serve strange gods, then he will turn and do you hurt, and consume you, after that he hath done you good. And the people said unto Joshua, Nay; but we will serve the Lord. And Joshua said unto the people, Ye are witnesses against yourselves that ye have chosen you the Lord, to serve him. And they said, We are witnesses." (Joshua 24:14-25.)

It will be remembered that Elijah gathered "all Israel"[2] on Mount Carmel that he might prove the power of Israel's God in contest with the priests of Baal and Ashteroth. "And Elijah came unto all the people, and said, How long halt ye between two opinions? If the Lord be God, follow him: but if Baal, then follow him." Elijah was to implore his God and the priests their gods to see which would send down fire from heaven to consume the bullock placed upon their respective altars. Ahab's and Jezebel's priests "prophesied [prayed and supplicated] until the time of the offering of the evening sacrifice," without effect. While they did so Elijah mocked them, suggesting that perhaps their god did not hear them because he was out walking, was preoccupied with business, or was sleeping. At the time of the evening sacrifice Elijah stood before the altar of Israel, which he had repaired, and implored the "Lord God of Abraham, Isaac, and of Israel" to make himself known. The fire of the Lord then "fell and consumed the burnt sacrifice, and the wood, and the stones, and the dust, and licked up the water that was in the trench," with which Elijah had drenched his offering. Thereafter, the four hundred and fifty priests of Baal (and we would assume the four hundred priests of Jezebel) were put to death, hardly a manifestation of an ecumenical spirit. (1 Kings 18:17–40; 19:1.) "They had committed the highest crime against the state and the people by introducing idolatry, and bringing down God's judgments upon the land; therefore their lives were forfeited to that [divine] law which had ordered every idolater to be slain."[3]

Nor is there any evidence that there was some acceptable latitude within the house of Israel relative to the doctrines of salvation. Christ in his ministry found no fellowship with any of the religious sects of his day. All were rejected and condemned. "This people draweth nigh unto me with their mouth, and honoureth me with their lips; but their heart is far from me," he said. "But in vain they do worship me, teaching for doctrines the commandments of men." (Matthew 15:8–9.) His warning to his disciples was that they "beware of the leaven [doctrines] of the Pharisees and of the Sadducees" (Matthew 16:6). In an exclusiveness typical of his prophets he testified: "I am the way, the truth, and the life: no man cometh unto the Father, but by me" (John 14:6).

"Truth is not a conflicting mass of confusion; it is not divergent views that are diametrically opposed to each other; it is not the vagaries and nonsense of sectarianism."[4] "There is no more self-evident truth in this world, there is nothing in all eternity more obvious than that there is and can be only one true Church. A true Church does not create itself any more than man creates God, or resurrects himself, or establishes for himself a celestial heaven. All churches may be false, but only one can be true, simply because religion comes from God, and God is not the author of confusion."[5]

Frequently various professing Christians show offense with Mormonism because of its bold announcement that it represents the "only true and living church upon the face of the whole earth" (D&C 1:30). Such an attitude is described as un-Christian, narrow-minded, and offensive. If those so complaining are Christian, they are in a theological position obligating them to say precisely the same thing to all non-Christian peoples, for if Jesus is "the way, the truth, and the life" there is no salvation save it be in his name. The profession of theological or ideological tolerance usually signals a sympathetic appreciation of everything except that which comes from contemporary prophets.

In its proper theological setting, tolerance, that is, patience and long-suffering, is something properly shown to people but not to doctrines. We cannot in the name of charity and kindness countenance ignorance or error. While we should by all means be gracious and kind to those who disagree with us, there is no salvation to be had in false doctrine.

The religion of true prophets always centers in a covenant message, a standard to be lived, rather than in supernatural experiences. The salvation proclaimed by the prophets of old was to be found in a way of life and not in religious experiences, as desirable as they may be. Nowhere in the scriptures do we find anyone professing salvation because he had a supernatural experience. Salvation is centered in the acceptance and living of the divine standard.

Our course of safety is in the daily living of gospel principles, not in marvelous manifestations. Cautioning Joseph Smith, the Lord said: "For although a man may have many revelations, and have power to do many mighty works, yet if he boasts in his own strength, and sets at naught the counsels of God, and follows after the dictates of his own will and carnal desires, he must fall and incur the vengeance of a just God upon him" (D&C 3:4). Again the Lord warned, "He that seeketh signs shall see signs, but not unto salvation. Verily, I say unto you, there are those among you who seek signs, and there have been such even from the beginning; but, behold, faith cometh not by signs, but signs follow those that believe. Yea, signs come by faith, not by the will of men, nor as they please, but by the will of God. Yea, *signs come by faith, unto mighty works,* for without faith no man pleaseth God; and with whom God is angry . . . he showeth no signs, only in wrath unto their condemnation." (D&C 63:7–11, italics added.)

The core of true religion is the prophet's surrender to God. Salvation is to be obtained on the Lord's terms and his only. The message is his and is therefore not subject to alteration or modification of any sort. It is the very fact that people are more important than principles (i.e., the word or the gospel) that makes principles (the gospel) more important than people. That is, since we can be saved only by obedience to the laws and ordinances of the gospel, to modify the gospel or deviate from its laws or ordinances in the supposed interest of an individual would be ultimately to condemn both the individual and the community, for we would have withheld from both of these the principles by which salvation comes. The designs and will of the prophet, no matter how well intended they may be, are of no moment. What is of importance is the message the prophet has been called to bear. That message must come to us in purity.

Christ is the perfect illustration of the principle. Repetitiously he made such comments as:

> The Son can do nothing of himself, but what he seeth the Father do: for what things soever he doeth, these also doeth the Son likewise (John 5:19).
>
> I can of mine own self do nothing: as I hear, I judge: and my judgment is just; because I seek not mine own will, but the will of the Father which hath sent me (John 5:30).
>
> For I came down from heaven, not to do mine own will, but the will of him that sent me (John 6:38).
>
> My doctrine is not mine, but his that sent me (John 7:16).
>
> I must work the works of him that sent me (John 9:4).
>
> If I do not the works of my Father, believe me not (John 10:37).

And he said, Abba, Father, all things are possible unto thee; take away this cup from me: nevertheless not what I will, but that thou wilt (Mark 14:36).

In all things Christ was submissive to the will of his Father. In the grand council when the Father had asked, "Whom shall I send?" his response had been, "Father, thy will be done, and the glory be thine forever" (Moses 4:2; Abraham 3:27). Such is our example and pattern, a pattern followed by all the holy prophets since the world began.

As to the charge given to those called in our dispensation, the Lord has consistently commanded that they proclaim the revelations of the Restoration and that they declare them as they received them. In his preface to the Doctrine and Covenants the Lord said, "Proclaim these things unto the world," having reference to that collection of revelations received by the Prophet Joseph Smith (D&C 1:17–19). To his early missionaries the Lord said, "Preach my gospel which ye have received, *even as ye have received it.*" To a missionary sent back to those from whom he had been converted the Lord said: "He may reason with them, *not according to that which he has received of them,* but according to that which shall be taught him by you my servants; and by so doing I will bless him, otherwise he shall not prosper." (D&C 49:1, 4, italics added.) Those in our dispensation who are sent to testify and warn the peoples of the world are to "proclaim the truth," the Lord said, "according to the revelations and commandments which I have given you"—meaning, the revelations given to Joseph Smith. "And thus, if ye are faithful," the Lord continued, "ye shall be laden with many sheaves, and crowned with honor, and glory, and immortality, and eternal life." (D&C 75:4–5.)

Thus those who are entitled to enjoy the spirit of prophecy and revelation are those who are true to the message they have been commissioned to deliver. There is a spirit associated with the message we have been called to proclaim that cannot be experienced when we have departed from the message. The word of the Lord, we are told, is "true and faithful" (D&C 66:11; Revelation 21:5), meaning that it is trustworthy and dependable. The true messenger must be equally loyal and trustworthy. To take license with the message is to offend that Spirit by which the message was revealed, and to lose the power by which it must be proclaimed. The core of true religion must ever be the submissiveness of the messenger to the message. He must speak as moved upon by the Holy Ghost. It is not a matter of what people want to hear, for the message is not of men but of God.

Characteristics of the Spirit of Revelation

As the message that is true has distinctive characteristics, so does the spirit that is to attest to its veracity, a spirit that is recognizable to those seeking truth and righteousness. Moroni, it will be remembered, promised that we might by the power of the Holy Ghost "know the truth of all things" (Moroni 10:5). Moroni did not promise that those possessing the spirit of prophecy would thus possess all truth, but rather that they would be granted a power of discernment by which they could in all matters of salvation clearly distinguish between truth and error. It is appropriate that those desiring that spirit be familiar with it that they might not be confused by counterfeit spirits. Distinctive characteristics of the Holy Ghost or the spirit of prophecy and revelation are as follows:

Selflessness. As Jesus said of himself, "I receive not honour from men" (John 5:41), so it must be said of the truths of heaven—they neither need nor seek the approbation of men. "Cursed is he," wrote Nephi, "that putteth his trust in man, or maketh flesh his arm, or shall hearken unto the precepts of men, save their precepts shall be given by the power of the Holy Ghost" (2 Nephi 28:31). The divine injunction to all who seek the wisdom of heaven is that they ask of God. The knowledge of heaven is not the province of scholars, the privilege of wealth, or the birthright of the chosen. Heaven's knowledge must be equally available to all—be they men, women, or children. All are invited to come to him, "the one like unto the other, and none are forbidden," for God does "nothing save it be plain unto the children of men; and he inviteth them all to come unto him and partake of his goodness; and he denieth none that come unto him." (2 Nephi 26:28, 33.)

Joy. The gospel is called the "glad tidings of great joy" (Mosiah 3:3; 4:11; Alma 13:22; D&C 31:3; Luke 2:10). It carries a spirit that lightens the heart and brings joy to the soul. The scriptures consistently describe those gathering to Zion —those coming to worship God—as doing so in the spirit of rejoicing and song. "The ransomed of the Lord shall return," Isaiah said, "and come to Zion with songs and everlasting joy upon their heads: they shall obtain joy and gladness, and sorrow and sighing shall flee away" (Isaiah 35:10; compare 55:12). It "filled me with unspeakable joy," Joseph Smith said in describing the feelings he experienced during the First Vision.[6] "My soul was filled with love and for many days I could rejoice with great joy and the Lord was with me."[7] The three words most common to the scriptural descriptions of those embracing the truths of salvation are *joy, gladness,* and *rejoicing.* Indeed, the gospel is the "oil of gladness" (Hebrews 1:9), the spirit of joy.

Peace. A companion to joy—one frequently found in the context of describing the spirit of the gospel or the presence of the Holy Ghost—is peace. Having promised his disciples the companionship of the Holy Ghost, Christ said: "Peace I leave with you, my peace I give unto you: not as the world giveth, give I unto you. Let not your heart be troubled, neither let it be afraid" (John 14:27). "The spirit of the devil produces confusion, disorder and misery," wrote Joseph Fielding, one of the first missionaries to the British Isles, while "the Spirit of God produces calmness, order and happiness."[8] The First Vision, it being our classic illustration, brought to Joseph Smith a "state of calmness and peace, indescribable."[9] George A. Smith said: "When a man's mind is illuminated by a dream, it leaves a vivid and pleasant impression; when it may be guided by the Spirit of God, it leaves the mind happy and comfortable, and the understanding clear."[10]

Uncertainty and fear characterize the spirit of men. Such was the reaction of Zacharias at the appearance of Gabriel (Luke 1:12), the Apostles in the upper room at the appearance of the resurrected Christ (Luke 24:37), and Joseph Smith when Moroni first appeared to him (Joseph Smith—History 1:32). "Fear not," Zacharias was told (Luke 1:13). "Peace be unto you" (Luke 24:36) was the Savior's expression to the Twelve. Joseph Smith's initial fear was dispelled, he said, by "a calmness and serenity of mind."[11]

Oliver Cowdery, in describing the restoration of the Aaronic Priesthood at the hands of John the Baptist, said that earth has not the "power to give the joy, to bestow the peace, or comprehend the wisdom which was contained in each sentence as they were delivered by the power of the Holy Spirit!"[12] Similarly, Gideon named the place where he stood face to face with the angel of the Lord as Jehovah-shalom, meaning the "peace of the Lord" (Judges 6:24).

When the Spirit of the Lord fell upon the people of King Benjamin "they were filled with joy, having received a remission of their sins, and having peace of conscience, because of the exceeding faith which they had in Jesus Christ" (Mosiah 4:3). Responding to Oliver Cowdery's request for spiritual confirmation, the Lord said: "Did I not speak peace to your mind concerning the matter? What greater witness can you have than from God?" (D&C 6:23.)

After his death, Joseph Smith appeared to Brigham Young in a dream and instructed him as follows: "Tell the people to be humble and faithful and be sure to keep the Spirit of the Lord and it will lead them right. Be careful and not turn away the still small voice; it will teach you what to do and where to go; it will yield the fruits of the kingdom. Tell the brethren to keep their hearts open to conviction, so that when the Holy Ghost comes to them, their hearts will be ready to receive it. They can tell the Spirit of the Lord from all other spirits—it will whisper peace and joy to their souls; it will take malice, hatred, strife and all evil from their hearts; and their whole desire will be to do good, bring forth righteousness and build up the kingdom of God."[13]

Enlightenment. To receive revelation is to receive light. As all revelation edifies, so all revelation enlightens. Truth shines. It enlightens both heart and mind. Enlightenment comes most frequently as the quickening of understanding or through "sudden strokes of ideas." Joseph Smith described the quickening of understanding as feeling "pure intelligence flowing into you."[14] "Sudden strokes of ideas" is more than just the turning on of a light where it was once dark; this process also causes existing lights to shine more brightly (D&C 8:2; 50:24; 88:6–12). The Apostle Paul defined the spirit of revelation as "the eyes of your understanding being enlightened" (Ephesians 1:18).

Virtue and purity. Another of the distinguishing characteristics of the revelations of heaven is "that there is no unrighteousness in them" (D&C 67:9). In describing the spirit of revelation, James wrote: "But the wisdom that is from above is first pure, then peaceable, gentle, and easy to be intreated, full of mercy and good fruits, without partiality, and without hypocrisy" (James 3:17). The word of God is a manifestation of the nature and character of God. As God cannot lack wisdom, so the revelations of heaven cannot be unwise; as God cannot lack virtue, purity, or any other godly attribute, so the revelations of heaven cannot lack these attributes. The spirit of revelation affects the heart and soul of man, not only creating an abhorrence for sin, but also giving birth to a "disposition . . . to do good continually." (Mosiah 5:2; Alma 13:12.)

Harmony. Truth does not contradict itself. God is not capricious or unreliable. All of heaven's truths sustain and support each other. The gospel is everlastingly the same. What the Lord says to one, he says to all (D&C 93:49). No one has ever received a revelation from heaven in which he was instructed to deny Christ, reject his prophets or their counsel, stray from the ordinances, or break gospel covenants. Never have the revelations of heaven excused any accountable souls from the obligation of obedience to the laws and ordinances of the gospel. This is the doctrine of kindred spirits or the verity that all things seek their own. "Intelligence cleaveth unto intelligence; wisdom receiveth wisdom; truth embraceth truth; virtue loveth virtue; light cleaveth unto light; mercy hath compassion on mercy and claimeth her own; justice continueth its course and claimeth its own; judgment goeth before the face of him who sitteth upon the throne and governeth and executeth all things" (D&C 88:40).

Warmth. Anyone who has found himself bearing testimony in a situation in which he had previously determined not to do so will find kinship with Jeremiah, who said that God's "word was in mine heart as a burning fire shut up in my bones, and I was weary with forbearing, and I could not stay [be constrained]" (Jeremiah 20:9). It is not uncommon for people to fail to identify the spirit of revelation. The traveling companions of the resurrected Christ on the Emmaus road realized only after the event that they had been tutored by that spirit. It was not until Christ left them that one turned to the other, saying, "Did not our heart burn with us, while he talked with us by the way, and while he opened to us the scriptures?" (Luke 24:32.) "Your bosom shall burn within you" the Lord told Joseph Smith, to confirm that which is proper and true (D&C 9:8).

Feelings. As all true religion brings with it a sense of confidence and assurance, so all true religion involves feelings. The first great revelation that Joseph Smith received came while he was reading the epistle of James. Joseph recorded the experience he had after pondering the promise that sincere seekers of the wisdom of heaven could obtain it through prayer: "Never did any passage of scripture come with more power to the heart of man than this did at this time to mine. It seemed to enter with great force into *every feeling of my heart.* I reflected on it again and again." (Joseph Smith—History 1:12, italics added.)

The spirit of revelation expresses itself most eloquently in the feelings of the heart. Christ taught that only those who "understood with their hearts" would be converted (Matthew 13:15). Teaching Joseph Smith how to recognize the spirit of revelation, the Savior said, "I will tell you in your mind and in your heart" (D&C 8:2), and promised, "you shall feel that it is right" (D&C 9:8). Consumed by a spirit of rebellion, Laman and Lemuel could not know that which must be spiritually discerned. Nephi said they were "past feeling," and therefore "could not feel his [the angel's] words" (1 Nephi 17:45). Paul defined such a state as mental vanity and "blindness of [the] heart." Like Nephi, Paul also used the expression "past feeling" to describe the state of those who had darkened their understanding by doing evil deeds (Ephesians 4:17–19).

If a doctrine is good, Joseph Smith taught, it will "taste good." "I can taste the principle of eternal life, and so can you," he said. "They are given to me by the revelations of Jesus Christ; and I know that when I tell you these words of eternal life as they are given to me, you taste them, and I know that you believe them. You say honey is sweet, and so do I. I can also taste the spirit of eternal life. I know it is good; and when I tell you of these things which were given me by inspiration of the Holy Spirit, you are bound to receive them as sweet, and rejoice more and more."[15] Alma describes the feelings associated with a knowledge of spiritual things as swelling motions which enlarge the soul and make the word become delicious to the taste (Alma 32:28).

Assuredness. The Spirit of the Lord is positive, not negative. Any doctrine of heaven properly taught and properly understood inspires and lifts, it gives us confidence and hope or, as Paul said, "much assurance" (1 Thessalonians 1:5). The plan of salvation was given to free the souls of men, not to bring them into bondage. Any doctrine that discourages or oppresses has either been mistaught or misunderstood.

Self-reliance. In the revelation given as a preface to the Doctrine and Covenants, the Lord testifies that the contents of the book are "true and faithful" (D&C 1:37). All that is revealed from heaven, be it institutional or personal revelation, is by its very nature "true and faithful." In this usage of the word the emphasis is not on truth as the opposite of falsehood but rather on truth as the essence of reliability. The truths of heaven are wholly dependable. The heavenly testimony continues: "What I the Lord have spoken, I have spoken, and I excuse not myself; and though the heavens and the earth pass away, my word shall not pass away, but shall all be fulfilled" (D&C 1:38).

Conclusion

Righteousness and truth are as longitude and latitude in charting the course that leads to eternal life. Only when the two are found in union can we plot a correct course. In all things we have the Holy Ghost as our guide, and by its power, we have been promised, we may know the truth of all things. Indeed, ours is the promise of the spirit of prophecy and revelation. "Ye are commanded," the Lord said, "in all things to ask of God, who giveth liberally; and that which the Spirit testifies unto you even so I would that ye should do in all holiness of heart, walking uprightly before me, considering the end of your salvation, doing all things with prayer and thanksgiving, that ye may not be seduced by evil spirits, or doctrines of devils, or the commandments of men; for some are of men, and others of devils" (D&C 46:7).

"The kingdom of God," Paul wrote, "is not meat and drink; but righteousness, and peace, and joy in the Holy Ghost" (Romans 14:17). This spirit was well known to the Psalmist, who wrote: "The law of the Lord is perfect, converting the soul: the testimony of the Lord is sure, making wise the simple. The statutes of the Lord are right, rejoicing the heart: the commandment of the Lord is pure, enlightening the eyes. The fear of the Lord is clean, enduring for ever: the judgments of the Lord are true and righteous altogether. More to be desired are they than gold, yea, than much fine gold: sweeter also than honey and the honeycomb. Moreover by them is thy servant warned: and in keeping of them there is great reward." (Psalm 19:7–11.)

Notes

1. Smith, *Lectures on Faith*, 4:13.
2. The reference must mean all the tribal heads and repre-

sentatives of each family. It is hard to suppose that "all Israel" were literally present.

3. Clarke, *Clarke's Commentary*, 2:460.

4. Bruce R. McConkie, *The Promised Messiah*, p. 338.

5. Bruce R. McConkie, *Doctrinal New Testament Commentary*, 2:506-7.

6. Backman, *Joseph Smith's First Vision*, p. 159.

7. Backman, *Joseph Smith's First Vision*, p. 157.

8. Fielding, *Diary of Joseph Fielding*, p. 8.

9. Backman, *Joseph Smith's First Vision*, p. 172; compare Orson Hyde's account, p. 175.

10. *Journal of Discourses*, 8:255.

11. *Messenger and Advocate*, 1:79.

12. *Messenger and Advocate*, 1:14-16; reprinted as a footnote at the end of Joseph Smith—History 1, in the Pearl of Great Price, p. 59 (1985 edition).

13. Watson, Manuscript History of Brigham Young, February 23, 1847.

14. *Teachings*, p. 151.

15. *Teachings*, p. 355.

10

Ye may all prophesy one by one, that all may learn, and all may be comforted.
—1 Corinthians 14:31

That All Might Prophesy

The spirit of prophecy is that spirit by which we know Jesus to be the Christ. It is a spirit that must be common to all of the household of faith. It is the breath of spiritual life, the light of heaven, and the only source by which the doctrines of salvation can be revealed or understood. It is the spirit by which scripture is spoken and written, and the spirit by which it must be interpreted and applied. It is the source of all spiritual understanding. To those who would teach the gospel the Lord has declared, "If ye receive not the Spirit ye shall not teach" (D&C 42:14), and in like manner well might it be said to those seeking to learn the gospel, "If ye receive not the Spirit ye shall not learn."

The Knowledge of God

Though the term is used with various shades of meaning, "to know God" in the purest scriptural sense is to have an intimate or covenant relationship with him. The Old Testament references to knowing God and to a man knowing his wife, meaning conceiving a child with her, both use the same Hebrew word (i.e., *yada*). As a man was to leave father and mother and cleave unto his wife and thus become one flesh with her, so he was to leave the things of the world and cleave unto his God and become one with him. As faithfulness in marriage was essential to the nurturing of love, so faithfulness in keeping gospel covenants was understood to be necessary in obtaining a knowledge of God. As love of spouse was strengthened in sacrifice and devotion, so the knowledge of God was obtained in living those covenants with exactness and honor. Thus a frequent characteristic of Hebrew prophecy was to describe apostasy through the metaphor of adultery, and Israel's covenant with God as a marriage (Jeremiah 2:20–37; Ezekiel 16; Hosea 1–3).

Similarly, we read in the New Testament that Joseph did not know Mary until after the birth of Christ (Matthew 1:25), and that it is life eternal to know God and Jesus Christ his Son (John 17:3). Both passages use the same Greek word, (i.e., *ginosko*). The *Dictionary of the New Testament* defines knowledge thus:

> Knowledge was not reducible to an act of the intellect that apprehended an object. The word preserves an experiential dimension that is characteristic of it: to observe, to experience, to know, to discern, to appraise, *to establish an intimate relationship between two persons, whence to choose, to elect, to enter a sexual union, finally, to recognize.* In conformity with this notion of truth, to know was to encounter someone; not to know was to thrust him aside from oneself. Knowledge of God was possible because this meant a "recognition" of the one who, through his creation, was already there. To know was to be disposed to obey.[1]

Again we see that fidelity was to love as righteousness was to the knowledge of God. Thus Peter lists such things as virtue, kindness, charity, and patience as requisites to knowing the Father and the Son. Independent of such attributes of godliness, all knowledge of God, he held, was "barren or unfruitful" (2 Peter 1:5–8). Texts in both the Old and the New Testament espouse the idea that one could not truly know God without that knowledge manifesting itself in the way one lived. (Deuteronomy 13:2–3; Jeremiah 22:15–16; Hosea 4:1–2; John 7:16–17.)

In Greek thought, by contrast, knowledge came through the senses and consisted of that which could be verified by observation. To the Greek, knowledge was the intellectual comprehension of the realities of the world. This was the knowledge of which Paul was so critical in his epistle to the Corinthians, the knowledge of which he said the "world by wisdom knew not God" (1 Corinthians 1:21). "The Greek thinkers supposed that they could grasp the nature of reality by applying rational processes to evaluate the data they gained by observing the universe. Paul says that the shape of reality can be known only through revelation, for God's Spirit must communicate the things known only to God. Some information about reality is simply not available to humanity through the senses, for 'No eye has seen, no ear has heard, no mind has conceived what God has prepared for those who love him.' "[2] (1 Corinthians 2:9.) Such was the knowledge of which Christ spoke, a knowledge which he said, "the world cannot receive" (John 14:17), a knowledge obtained only through obedience (John 7:17).

This idea of sacred knowledge being obtainable only in the living of sacred covenants finds eloquent expression in the revelations of the Restoration. It was in the restoration of the Melchizedek Priesthood that we obtained "the key of the knowledge of God" (D&C 84:19), and it is a revelation concerning the priesthood in which we are told that the attributes of godliness are requisite for obtaining that knowledge (D&C 107:30–31). Further, we are told that all such knowledge must come by revelation (D&C 121:26), and that its nature is such that it cannot be understood by the "carnal mind" (D&C 67:12; Alma 36:4). The plan of salvation, or "pure knowledge" (D&C 121:42), as modern revelation calls it, must have heaven as its source (D&C 50:13–20), and is to "descend" upon us as the "dews of Carmel" (D&C 128:19; 121:45). It is the knowledge which has been hidden from the world (D&C 89:19), that rises with us in the resurrection. It is a knowledge obtained only in the classrooms of "diligence and obedience" (D&C 130:18–19).

What Is Truth?

Like *knowledge,* the word *truth* also carries a richer and deeper meaning in the scriptures than is generally accorded it. Our word *true* is derived from the Old English "treowe," which meant "faithful," "trustworthy," or "covenant."[3] To be true was to be "constant," "steadfast," and "faithful." The standard dictionary of Joseph Smith's day stated that "the primary sense of the root is to make close and fast, to set, or to stretch, strain, and thus make straight and close."[4] This understanding gives greater meaning to the testimony of Nephi in which he speaks of the words of Christ as being "true and faithful" (2 Nephi 31:15), or to the testimony of the Lord himself in which he declared that the prophecies and promises in the Doctrine and Covenants "are true and faithful" (D&C 1:37). That is, they are trustworthy, and obedient acceptance of them constitutes a covenant with God which he cannot break (D&C 82:10).

In the Hellenistic or Greek tradition truth comes from a root meaning "to be hidden," and thus came to signify the unveiling of reality. In Semitic tradition, however, it meant to be solid or stable; one who was truthful was one who could be trusted.[5] For the Greek, the opposite of truth was error or deception, while for the household of faith truth was light, and its opposite consisted of the breaking of covenants with God. Truth was something to be done rather than something to be learned. Thus we find the Savior reasoning that he who does evil "hateth the light, neither cometh to the light," that his deeds might be hidden, while "he that *doeth* truth cometh to the light, that his deeds may be made manifest, that they are wrought in God." (John 3:20–21, italics added.) Again John writes: "God is light, and in him is no darkness at all. If we say that we have fellowship with him, and walk in darkness, we lie, and *do not* the truth." (1 John 1:5–6, italics added.)

Of the Gospel writers, it is John who uses the word *truth* in its highest spiritual sense. John, for instance, preserves the Savior's self-characterization that he is "the way, the truth, and the life" and that no man can come unto the Father but through him (John 14:6). The testimony of John's Gospel is that Christ is light, that light is truth, that salvation is in truth, and that we obtain salvation by acquiring light and truth. Thus salvation is the process of becoming Christlike; it is the process of learning to think as he thought, feel as he felt, and do as he did.

The scholar can define the gospel as "all truth," but the prophet cannot. Prophetic knowledge is not the result of abstract learning. It is not a mastery of theosophic principles or subtle theories. It is something found more naturally in service than in sequestered study. It is more the product of calloused hands than of a furrowed brow. It is more the child of the simple heart than the sire of eloquence of speech. It is something that rests closer to the heart than to the intellect.

The Doctrine and Covenants is commonly quoted to establish a definition of truth as a "knowledge of things as they are, and as they were, and as they are to come." This completes neither the sentence nor the thought. The record continues, stating that "whatsoever is more or less than this is the spirit of that wicked one who was a liar from the beginning." (D&C 93:24–25.) The thrust of the revelation is that divine truth is neither to be embellished nor pruned. It is not in the province of man to add to or take from the gospel message. The revelation continues by stating that no man can receive the fulness of such truths without keeping the commandments, while the person who keeps the commandments is promised that he will "receive truth and light," until he is "glorified in truth and knoweth all things" (D&C 93:27–28). It is an experiential knowledge of which the revelation speaks. As we cannot describe colors to a man born blind, so we cannot convey the truths of heaven to those who have not been born of the Spirit.

If by *truth* we have in mind merely "accurate information," truth is as much the servant of sin as it is the friend of righteousness. As there are no wars in which brothers have not been called upon to fight each other, so the great conflict between the sons of darkness and the sons of light finds such *truth* (information) a weapon common to both armies. Soldiers in both camps quote scriptures, profess a love of God, and claim a heritage of dreams and revelations, of prophets and angels. If angels be our illustration, we note that the scriptures generally assume the responsibility to identify an angel's nature. This is particularly true of Bible texts. The scriptural pattern is to say that "an angel of the Lord," "an angel of God," or "an angel of his presence" appeared with a message. It is not enough that it be an angel; it must be an angel from the divine presence. So it is with truth. Truth alone has no salvation in it. Again we note from the scriptural pattern that truth must have its proper companions. Common scriptural phrases are:

"goodness and truth"
"sincerity and truth"
"kindness and truth"
"mercy and truth"
"right and truth"
"peace and truth"
"light and truth"
"truth and meekness"
"truth and uprightness"
"faithfulness and truth"
"truth and righteousness"
"grace and truth"
"spirit and in truth"
"truth and soberness"
"truth in the law"
"truth and holiness"
"goodness, righteousness, and truth"
"grace, equity, and truth"
"wisdom, mercy, and truth"

Accurate information is one thing, the *truths* of salvation entirely another. Those who have interpreted the marvelous statement that "the glory of God is intelligence" to mean that salvation is found in the accumulation of knowledge, or even that it is found in living in harmony with correct principles, have missed the point of the revelation. Let us read it again: "The glory of God is intelligence, *or, in other words, light and truth. Light and truth forsake that evil one.*" (D&C 93:36–37, italics added.) The *truths* of salvation do not stand alone. As Paul said, "neither is the man without the woman, neither the woman without the man, in the Lord" (1 Corinthians 11:11), so might it be said, "neither is truth without light, nor light without truth, in the Lord." As Joseph Smith taught that one cannot have faith without its "train of attendants"—meaning "apostles, prophets, evangelists, pastors, teachers, gifts, wisdom, knowledge, miracles, healings, tongues, interpretation of tongues, etc."[6] so it ought to be said that one cannot have truth without *its* train of attendants, meaning goodness, mercy, peace, uprightness, faithfulness, grace, holiness, light, and so on.

The statement that "it is impossible for a man to be saved in ignorance" has no reference to the importance of our knowing math, science, or languages. The knowledge of such was not necessary for Joseph Smith to open the heavens, nor did their mastery have anything to do with Abraham, Isaac, and Jacob obtaining their exaltation. The scriptural text has specific reference to ignorance of the "more sure word of prophecy," and to the simple declaration that there is no salvation without revelation (D&C 131:5–6).[7] Again Joseph Smith is quoted as saying, "A man is saved no faster than he gets knowledge." In so stating, however, the Prophet made no reference to the kinds of things contained in a college curriculum, valuable as these may be for some purposes. His attention was centered on the loss of "light and truth" that results from disobedience (see D&C 93:39). "The Church," he said, "must be cleansed, and I proclaim against all iniquity. *A man is saved no faster than he gets knowledge,* for if he does not get knowledge, he will be brought into captivity by some evil power in the other world, as evil spirits will have more knowledge, and consequently more power, than many men who are on the earth. *Hence it needs revelation to assist us, and give us knowledge of the things of God.*"[8]

The church or kingdom of God is more than a library containing all knowledge. God is appreciably more than simply the universe's most intelligent being. Salvation consists of more than a doctor's degree in eternal principles. As the best of soil is of no value in producing good fruit without light and water, so truth independent of the attributes of godliness has no power to exalt. Nor is there any equality among truths. Some have within them the power of salvation; some have not. Some are of infinite importance; others are of little more than passing interest. That Peter, James, and John literally heard the voice of the Father bearing witness that Jesus of Nazareth was his Son is a matter of considerable importance; whether at that time the three Apostles stood on Mount Tabor or Mount Hermon is of little moment. That all truths can be circumscribed into one great whole is a verity of heaven, but to suppose that a knowledge of math or science brings a remission of sins misses the whole point of the gospel.

Those singular truths that constitute the gospel of salvation must bear the label of revelation and can only be taught by one who has been properly called and authorized. Of necessity they must be taught by the spirit of revelation and must learn by that same spirit. By definition, any principle that does not require the light of heaven—that is, any principle that can be taught by the learned and the wise independent of the spirit of revelation—is not a principle of salvation. Heaven's truths require both teacher and student to be clothed in the robes of righteousness. Indeed, without such truths there is no righteousness.

The Meaning of Righteousness

In the context of the Old Testament the word *righteous* means "to be right," or "to be in the right"; synonyms are *straight* and *just*.[9] Likewise, in the New Testament *righ-*

teousness is defined as "the character or quality of being right or just; it was formerly spelled 'rightwiseness,' which clearly expresses the meaning."[10] That is, to be righteous was to be both right and wise.

As used in the scriptures, righteousness centers in doing that which is just and lawful. Jesus, for instance, though he was without sin, could not "fulfill all righteousness" without being baptized (2 Nephi 31:5). So it is with all men. Joseph Smith taught that "if a man gets a fullness of the priesthood of God he has to get it in the same way that Jesus Christ obtained it, and that was by keeping all the commandments and obeying all the ordinances of the house of the Lord."[11] Thus in the scriptural sense righteousness, truth, and knowledge are all attributes of Deity, not commodities. They describe the nature of God rather than the glories with which he has surrounded himself.

The Gospel Covenant

In the context of the scriptures the "gospel" is tightly defined. This is the reason why Moroni spoke of the Book of Mormon as containing the "fulness of the everlasting Gospel" (Joseph Smith—History 1:34) and why the Lord declared it to contain the "fulness of the gospel of Jesus Christ" (D&C 20:9). No one would suppose that the Book of Mormon contained all the truths of science, math, chemistry, or medicine, or even all religious truths. Surely the mind of God cannot be conscribed to a book. What it contains is a faithful or trustworthy declaration of the covenant of salvation.

In defining that covenant of salvation, knowledge, truth, and righteousness are used in a refined and disciplined manner. As the scriptures are narrow in their definition of the gospel, so they are in the usage of these companion words. When the Savior said, "know the truth and the truth shall make you free," he was not referring to a freedom that accrued from the accumulation of information. Christ was addressing himself to those "who believed in him." To them, and to them alone, the promise was given that if they continued to believe that which he taught them, they would then know the truth—meaning, the truths of salvation. Those truths and those truths alone would free them from the darkness of sin and the chains of hell. (John 8:30–32.) The unanswered question of Pilate to Christ, "What is truth?" is often quoted. What has not received proper attention is the Savior's testimony that preceded it. "To this end was I born," he said, "and for this cause came I into the world, that I should bear witness unto the truth. Every one that is of the truth heareth my voice." (John 18:37.) To know the truth is to know the voice of the Lord; it is to possess the spirit of prophecy and revelation.

Witnesses of Christ

Baptism is the gate by which all accountable persons enter the kingdom of God. No baptism is of efficacy, virtue, and force unless it is performed under the direction of the keys and authority of the priesthood. The ordinance itself consists of two parts: the immersion in water and the immersion in the Spirit. The outward or water baptism signifies that one has been washed clean from sin and transgression. The inward or spiritual ordinance, which is accomplished by the laying on of hands and the conferring of the gift of the Holy Ghost, completes the sanctifying act of the water baptism and grants the one baptized the right to companionship with the Holy Ghost. In addition to his role as a sanctifier, the Holy Ghost is a testator, revelator, and teacher. Hence Joseph Smith's statements that "no man can receive the Holy Ghost without receiving revelations,"[12] and that "no man can know that Jesus is the Lord, but by the Holy Ghost."[13]

All baptized members of the Church assume the obligation to be witnesses of Christ and verifiers of his gospel. In baptism we covenant "to stand as witnesses of God at all times and in all things, and in all places" that we may be in, "even until death." In turn, the Lord promises to "pour out his Spirit" in abundance upon us. (Mosiah 18:9–10.) That covenant promise with its attendant blessings is of such importance that we are invited to renew it regularly in the partaking of the sacrament. In the sacramental prayer we announce our willingness to take upon us the name of Christ, to "always remember him and keep his commandments," and then are assured that by so doing we may always have his Spirit to be with us (D&C 20:77).

Thus all who hold citizenship in the kingdom of God are to be witnesses of its King and advocates of its doctrines. All are to be special witnesses. Emphasizing this point, Wilford Woodruff addressed himself to the Twelve Apostles, the seventy apostles, the high priest apostles, and all other apostles. He charged all with the testimony of Christ to rise to the responsibility of that marvelous spiritual witness.[14] More than two years before the office of Apostle was restored, the Lord said to Joseph Smith and the other brethren of the Church, "You are mine apostles, even God's high priests; ye are they whom my Father hath given me; ye are my friends; therefore, as I said unto mine apostles I say unto you again, that every soul who believeth on your words, and is baptized by water for the remission of sins, shall receive the Holy Ghost" (D&C 84:63–64). By contrast, the Lord said, "But with some I am not well pleased, for they will not open their mouths, but they hide the talent which I have given unto them, because of the fear of man. Wo unto such, for mine anger is kindled against them." (D&C 60:2.) To fail to bear testimony of that which we know to be true is to place ourselves under condemnation (D&C 67:8).

Heirs of the Spirit of Prophecy and Revelation

There is no distinction made in the covenant of baptism between men, women, and children. All receive the same promise of a remission of sins, all are directed to receive the Holy Ghost, and each has a rightful claim to a spiritual gift or gifts (D&C 46:10–11). If the ministry of angels be the example, the scriptural writ announces that God "imparteth his word by angels unto men, yea, not only men but women also. Now this is not all; little children do have words given unto them many times, which confound the wise and the learned." (Alma 32:23.)

All who are upon the errand of the Lord are commanded to "speak as they are moved upon by the Holy Ghost." With that command comes the assurance that "whatsoever they shall speak when moved upon by the Holy Ghost shall be scripture, shall be the will of the Lord, shall be the mind of the Lord, shall be the word of the Lord, shall be the voice of the Lord, and the power of God unto salvation." (D&C 68:3-4.) Significantly, some of our greatest scriptural texts come from faithful souls who held no position of authority in the Church.

Women Who Have Spoken Scripture

After the Fall and the expulsion from the Garden of Eden, Eve, by the spirit of revelation, made one of the most perceptive declarations of the plan of salvation ever to have come from mortal lips: "Were it not for our transgression," she said, "we never should have had seed, and never should have known good and evil, and the joy of our redemption, and the eternal life which God giveth unto all the obedient" (Moses 5:11). While the Holy Ghost rested upon her, Mary responded to Elisabeth's inspired salutation by uttering the memorable words since adopted as part of the musical ritual of many churches under the latin name, the Magnificat. This is an inspired psalm of praise, worship, and thanksgiving. (Luke 1:46-55.)

As there were prophetesses in Old and New Testament days, so there are in our own. Though such names as Mary Fielding Smith and Eliza R. Snow immediately suggest themselves, our dispensation has known countless women of like spiritual stature. They are the mothers of faithful missionaries, the role models of faithful daughters, the wives of men who honor their priesthood, and they are teachers and leaders of unsurpassed inspiration. They dream dreams, see visions, entertain angels, prophesy, and speak by the spirit of revelation. Most of what they do and have done is known only within the circle of their own families. We do not know how many prophetesses there were in the city of Enoch or among the righteous Nephites or in other eras among faithful Saints. We do know that the need for prophetesses is as great as the need for prophets, for as Paul said: "Neither is the man without the woman, neither the woman without the man, in the Lord" (1 Corinthians 11:11). Luke tells us that Philip had four daughters, all of whom had the gift of prophecy (Acts 21:8–9); doubtless many other women in the meridian church did also, for such has always been the pattern among those of households of faith.

Lay Members Speak Scripture

The first public witnesses of the birth of Christ were lowly shepherds of Judea. If they were not the first to bear testimony of his birth and divine sonship within the walls of the temple, the humble old Simeon, to whom the birth of Christ had been revealed by the Holy Ghost, was. In either case it was Simeon who first identified the Christ in the temple and prophesied of his ministry and the sorrow which Mary would yet know (Luke 2:25–35). Though apparently neither Mark nor Luke held any office or position in the meridian Church other than that of missionary, we are indebted to them for much of our New Testament record. They are responsible for sixty-eight chapters of the New Testament: the books of Mark, Luke, and Acts. Only Paul contributed more to the New Testament record than did Luke.

In all of this there is a message of considerable importance. It is not for our ordained prophets to write all the inspired books, poetry, plays, or music in the Church. It is not for them to give all the patriarchal blessings, deliver all the inspired addresses, teach all the classes, or lead all the choirs. Indeed, it may never be their lot to paint the great paintings, sculpture with inspiration, or design chapels and temples. The kingdom of God is to be built as the tabernacle in the wilderness or the temple in Jerusalem was built—that is, by the revelation of God as it manifests itself through a prophet and a nation of artists and craftsmen. All who labor to build the house of the Lord, be it temporal or spiritual, be it ancient or modern, are to do so with the spirit of revelation. And ought it not be said that, as the greatest of temples awaits building, so the best of books, music, art, and all things that testify of our God still await the day of their creation?

The Spirit of Revelation: Its Branches and Fruits

"Those who preach by the power of the Holy Ghost use the scriptures as their basic source of knowledge and doctrine," observed Elder Bruce R. McConkie. "They begin with what the Lord has before revealed to other inspired men. But it is the practice of the Lord to give added knowledge to those upon whose hearts the true meanings and intents of the scriptures have been impressed. Many great doctrinal revelations come to those who preach from the scriptures. When they are in tune with the infinite, the Lord lets them know, first, the full and complete meaning of the scriptures they are expounding, and then he ofttimes expands their views so that new truths flood in upon them, and they learn added things that those who do not follow such a course can never know."[15] This explains why we have been instructed to preach "none other things than that which the prophets and apostles have written, and that which is taught [us] by the Comforter through the prayer of faith" (D&C 52:9). That is, when we begin with the words of "the prophets and apostles," when their words become our guide and their spirit a source of strength, we can climb the mountains that they climbed, we can see as they saw, and we can continue to climb.

No revelation can be properly understood unless it is read in the same spirit by which it was given. When that spirit sustains its reading it becomes as a living vine or as the tree of life—it obtains a newness of life—its branches can reach further and yield fruit in greater measure than it previously did. Thus the Lord can give a revelation with the promise that those who read it at subsequent times, doing so by the power of his Spirit, can testify that they have heard his voice (D&C 18:34–36). Such was Alma's testimony—having prayerfully read and pondered the scriptures available to him, he testified, saying: "It has . . . been revealed unto me, that the words which have been spoken by our fathers are true, even so according to the spirit of prophecy which is in me, which is also by the manifestation of the Spirit of God" (Alma 5:47).

Similarly, we have listened as a modern Apostle stood to testify of Christ and his atonement, saying: "In speaking of these wondrous things I shall use my own words, though you may think they are the words of scripture, words spoken by other Apostles and prophets. True it is they were first proclaimed by others, but they are now mine, for the Holy Spirit of God has borne witness to me that they are true, and it is now as though the Lord has revealed them to me in the first instance. I have thereby heard his voice and know his word."[16]

When the tree of revelation is properly nourished it can bring forth fresh fruits with every reading, and all within the household of faith are invited to feast from it. The promise of the Savior was that all who hunger and thirst after the fruits of righteousness "shall be filled with the Holy Ghost" (3 Nephi 12:6). Thus the promise of the spirit of prophecy and revelation is extended to all who properly seek it.

The Restoration of All Things

It is the promise of the scriptures that an apostasy that was to be universal was to be followed by a restoration equally expansive. In the fullest sense, the Restoration will not be complete until the earth and all things on it are returned to the pristine state known in Edenic days. This will be a glorious day when the veil "which hideth the earth, shall be taken off, and all flesh shall see me together," the Lord promised. "And every corruptible thing, both of man, or of the beasts of the field, or of the fowls of the heavens, or of the fish of the sea, that dwells upon all the face of the earth, shall be consumed; and also that of element shall melt with fervent heat; and all things shall become new, and my knowledge and glory may dwell upon all the earth." (D&C 101:23–25.) Such will be the day spoken of by Christ when he said, "Every plant, which my heavenly Father hath not planted, shall be rooted up" (Matthew 15:13). Though all corruptible things in our telestial earth are to be consumed as it receives again its paradisiacal glory, Christ's attention in making this statement was more precisely directed to the spiritual darkness of his day. The doctrines, philosophies, and ideologies born of the mind, all that blinds a man to the revelations of heaven, are to be rooted up. It was not *jihad*, or holy war, of which the Savior spoke; it was not the work of oppression or of the sword. Rather, he promised that the day would come when the light of heaven would chase every shadow of error and falsehood away. It was a change of seasons that was promised, a time when the warmth and light of the summer sun would melt the winter's snow and invite all that was good to lift its head and arms toward heaven again.

With the restoration of the gospel through the Prophet Joseph Smith we are privileged to enjoy the splendor of the spring that precedes the summer of millennial glory. Ours is a day of pruning and preparation. It is a day in which much work needs to be done and the laborers are few. All have suffered in the long winter's night. It was not just the temple flock that went without proper fodder. All the earth's inhabitants have shivered and hungered and longed for a better day. The artist, writer, composer, scientist, and educator are all to be blessed by the light of the Restoration. Indeed, it is a restoration of all things that we seek.

A Personal Gospel Dispensation

A gospel dispensation is a period of time in which the gospel in its purity is revealed anew from the heavens. Ours is the dispensation of the fulness of times, meaning that in our case the Lord has seen fit to restore to us every key, knowledge, power, authority, and glory that has ever been enjoyed by the Saints in ages past. All that we have we have received at their hands, and like the children of wise parents we have been prepared to stand independent. We make no claim upon the Bible for our doctrine, for we have it by direct revelation. We are not indebted to scholars or universities for our priesthood or authority, for we trace it to the Lord himself. We stand independent. We have no doctrines, keys, powers, or authorities that we do not claim directly from heaven itself.

As the Church stands independent of the world, so must we. As the Church has power innate to itself, so must we have power innate to ourselves. As the Church is guided by the spirit of revelation, so must our lives be guided by that same spirit. The Church is but the pattern for the family and the individual. As the gospel has been dispensed by revelation to the Church, so it must be dispensed by revelation to each member within it. Another man's baptism will not remit our sins, nor will his knowledge, faith, or righteousness save us. There is no collective salvation, nor will there be a mass judgment. All must stand independent; all must know for themselves, all must have a personal gospel dispensation and come to know the spirit of prophecy and revelation.

Final Conclusions

1. There is but one plan of salvation. We do not have one doctrine for prophets and another doctrine for the masses of people. Neither do we have one doctrine for men and another doctrine for women. All who obtain salvation will do so by obedience to the same laws and the same ordinances. "What I say unto one I say unto all," the Lord declared (D&C 93:49). All are entitled to faith in equal measure, and all have equal claim to the attention of heaven and an inheritance therein.

2. Prophets, those with the spirit of prophecy and revelation, are but the pattern; they are but illustrations or examples of what all the children of the Father are expected to be. Whatever spiritual endowment they have received, all are entitled to receive. The manner in which God converses with them is but the prototype of the manner in which God will converse with each of his children. Similarly, that devotion and sacrifice required of the prophets ought also to be the common lot of all the faithful Saints. Such is the justice of heaven; such is the doctrine of salvation.

3. We do not have one doctrine or standard for those who have been ordained prophets and another of lesser order for the rest of the children of God. All are invited to come unto the Father and receive of his fulness. Our baptism does not differ from that of our prophets, nor does our priesthood, or our endowment. We have made the same covenants and we have received the same promises. There is no knowledge in the realm of eternal truths to which they have greater claim than we. "The Spirit itself beareth witness with our spirit," Paul testified, "that we are the children of God: and if children, then heirs; heirs of God, and joint-heirs with Christ; if so be that we suffer with him, that we may be also glorified together" (Romans 8:16–17). There are no promises or blessings to which all the children of God do not have equal claim. Through faith and obedience all have the promise that they may be equal with their God in "power, and in might, and in dominion" (D&C 76:94–95).

Notes

1. Leon-Dufour, *Dictionary of the New Testament*, p. 259, italics added.
2. Richards, *Expository Dictionary of Bible Words*, p. 386.
3. Partridge, *Origins: A Short Etymological Dictionary of Modern English*, p. 740.
4. *Noah Webster's First Edition of an American Dictionary of the English Language.*
5. Leon-Dufour, *Dictionary of the New Testament*, p. 412.

6. Smith, *Lectures on Faith*, 7:20.
7. *Teachings*, p. 160.
8. *Teachings*, p. 217, italics added.
9. Wilson, *Old Testament Word Studies*, p. 357.
10. Vine, *An Expository Dictionary of New Testament Words*, p. 298.
11. *Teachings*, p. 308.
12. *Teachings*, p. 328.
13. *Teachings*, p. 223.
14. *Journal of Discourses*, 4:147.
15. Bruce R. McConkie, *The Promised Messiah*, pp. 515–16.
16. Bruce R. McConkie, Conference Report, April 1985, p. 9.

Bibliography

Archer, Gleason L. *Encyclopedia of Bible Difficulties.* Grand Rapids, Michigan: Zondervan Publishing House, 1982.

Arrington, Leonard J. *Brigham Young: American Moses.* New York: Alfred A. Knopf, 1985.
Michigan: Zondervan Publishing House, 1982.

Aune, David E. *Prophecy in Early Christianity and the Ancient Mediterranean World.* Grand Rapids, Michigan: William B. Eerdmans Publishing Co., 1983.

Backman, Milton V., Jr. *Joseph Smith's First Vision.* Salt Lake City: Bookcraft, 1980.

Barr, James. *Holy Scripture: Canon, Authority, Criticism.* Philadelphia: The Westminster Press, 1983.

Barthel, Manfred. Translated and adapted by Mark Howson. *What the Bible Really Says.* New York: William Morrow and Company, Inc., 1982.

"The Book of the Revelation of Abraham." *Improvement Era.* The Church of Jesus Christ of Latter-day Saints, 1:10, 1898:715.

Bruce, F. F. *Second Thoughts on the Dead Sea Scrolls.* Grand Rapids, Michigan: William B. Eerdmans Publishing Co., 1972.

Butterworth, G. W., trans. *Origen on First Principles.* Gloucester, Massachusetts: 1973.

Buttric, George Arthur, ed. *The Interpreter's Bible.* 12 vols. Nashville: Abingdon Press, 1971.

Charlesworth, James H. *The Old Testament Pseudepigrapha*, 2 vols. Garden City, New York: Doubleday and Company, Inc., 1983.

Clarke, Adam, LL. D., F. S. A. *Clarke's Commentary.* 3 vols. Nashville: Abingdon Press, no date given.

Conference Report. Salt Lake City: The Church of Jesus Christ of Latter-day Saints, October 1925, April 1985.

Edersheim, Alfred. *The Life and Times of Jesus the Messiah.* Grand Rapids, Michigan: William B. Eerdmans Publishing Co., 1890.

Ehat, Andrew F. and Lyndon W. Cook, ed. *The Words of Joseph Smith.* Provo, Utah: Religious Studies Center, Brigham Young University, 1980.

Esplin, Ronald K. "A Great Work Done in That Land." *Ensign*. Salt Lake City: The Church of Jesus Christ of Latter-day Saints, July 1987, pp. 20–27.

Fielding, Joseph. *Diary of Joseph Fielding*. Harold B. Lee Library, Brigham Young University, Provo, Utah.

Gaster, Theodor H., trans. *The Dead Sea Scriptures*. Garden City, New York: Anchor Press/Doubleday, 1976.

Ginzberg, Louis. *The Legends of the Jews*. 7 vols. Philadelphia: The Jewish Publication Society of America, 1912–1928.

Harris, R. Laird, Gleason L. Archer, Jr., and Bruce K. Waltke. *Theological Wordbook of the Old Testament*. 2 vols. Chicago: Moody Press, 1980.

Hatch, Edwin. *The Influence of Greek Ideas on Christianity*. Gloucester, Massachusetts: Peter Smith, 1970.

Hennecke, Edgar. *New Testament Aprocrypha*. Wilhelm Schneemelcher, ed. R. Mcl. Wilson, trans. Philadelphia: The Westminster Press, 1964.

Heschel, Abraham J. *The Prophets*. 2 vols. New York: Harper Torchbooks, 1969.

Jenson, Andrew. *Historical Record*. 9 vols. Salt Lake City: Andrew Jenson, 1889.

Journal of Discourses. 26 vols. Liverpool: F.D. Richards and Sons, 1851–1886.

King, Edward G. *The Yalkut on Zechariah*. Cambridge: Deighton, Bell and Co., 1882.

Kittel, Gerhard and Gerhard Friedrich. Trans. Geoffrey W. Bromiley. *Theological Dictionary of the New Testament*. Grand Rapids, Michigan: William B. Eerdmans Publishing Co., 1985.

Klausner, Joseph. *The Messianic Idea in Israel*. London: George Allen and Unwin Ltd, 1956.

Kubo, Sakae and Walter F. Specht. *So Many Versions?* Grand Rapids, Michigan: Zondervan Publishing House, 1983.

Leon-Dufour, Xavier. Trans. Terrence Prendergast. *Dictionary of the New Testament*. San Francisco: Harper and Row, 1983.

Martin, Walter. *The New Cults*. Ventura, California: Regal Books, 1980.

McConkie, Bruce R. *A New Witness for the Articles of Faith*. Salt Lake City: Deseret Book Co., 1982.

———. *The Millennial Messiah*. Salt Lake City: Deseret Book Co., 1982.

———. *Mormon Doctrine*, 2nd ed. Salt Lake City: Bookcraft, 1966.

———. *Doctrinal New Testament Commentary*. 3 vols. Salt Lake City: Bookcraft, 1965–1973.

———. *The Promised Messiah*. Salt Lake City: Deseret Book Co., 1978.

———. Unpublished talk given to prospective Book of Mormon teachers at BYU. June 13, 1984.

McConkie, Joseph Fielding. *His Name Shall Be Joseph*. Salt Lake City: Hawkes Publishing Inc., 1980.

———. "Premortal Existence, Foreordinations, and Heavenly Councils." *Aprocryphal Writings and the Latter-day Saints*. C. Wilfred Griggs, ed. Provo, Utah: Brigham Young University, Religious Studies Center, 1986.

———. *The Spirit of Revelation*. Salt Lake City: Deseret Book Co., 1984.

McConkie, Joseph Fielding and Robert L. Millet. *Doctrinal Commentary on the Book of Mormon*. 4 vols. Salt Lake City: Bookcraft, 1987–.

Messenger and Advocate. Kirtland, Ohio: The Church of Jesus Christ of Latter-day Saints, 1834–1835.

Milgrom, Jacob. "The Dead Sea Temple Scroll." *Scriptures for the Modern World*. Provo, Utah: Brigham Young University, Religious Studies Center, 1984.

Napier, B. N. "Prophet, Prophetism." *Interpreter's Dictionary of the Bible*. 5 vols. Nashville: Abingdon Press, 1962.

The New English Bible, 2nd ed. Oxford: Oxford University Press, 1970.

Nibley, Hugh. "The Passing of the Church." *When the Lights Went Out: Three Studies on the Ancient Apostasy*. Salt Lake City: Deseret Book Co., 1970.

Paine, Thomas. *Common Sense*. Great Britain: Cox and Wyman Ltd., 1985.

———. *The Age of Reason, Part 1*. New York: The Bobbs-Merrill Co., Inc., 1957.

Partridge, Eric. *Origins: A Short Etymological Dictionary of Modern English*. New York: Greenwich House, distributed by Crown Publishers, Inc., 1983.

Richards, Lawrence O. *Expository Dictionary of Bible Words*. Grand Rapids, Michigan: Zondervan Publishing House, Regency Reference Library, 1985.

Ricks, Stephen D. "No Prophet Is Accepted in His Own Country." *The Gospels.* Vol. 5 of *Studies in Scripture.* Kent P. Jackson and Robert L. Millet, eds. Salt Lake City: Deseret Book Co., 1986.

Robinson, Stephen E. "The Setting of the Gospels." *The Gospels.* Vol. 5 of *Studies in Scripture.* Kent P. Jackson and Robert L. Millet, eds. Salt Lake City: Deseret Book Co., 1986.

Schaff, Philip and Henry Wace, eds. *Nicene and Post-Nicene Fathers of the Christian Church.* 14 vols. Grand Rapids, Michigan: William B. Eerdmans Publishing Company.

Schultz, Joseph P. "Angelic Opposition to the Ascension of Moses and the Revelation of the Law." *The Jewish Quarterly Review,* Vol. 61, April 1971, no. 4.

Smith, Joseph, Jr. *History of the Church,* 7 vols. Roberts, Brigham H., comp. Salt Lake City: The Church of Jesus Christ of Latter-day Saints, 1932–1951.

──────. *Lectures on Faith.* Salt Lake City: Deseret Book Co., 1983.

──────. *Teachings of the Prophet Joseph Smith.* Joseph Fielding Smith, comp. Salt Lake City: Deseret Book Co., 1976.

Smith, Joseph F. Minutes of the Council of Fifty, April 21, 1880. Cited in Robert L. Millet, "The Development of the Concept of Zion in Mormon Theology," doctoral dissertation, Florida State University, 1983.

Smith, Joseph Fielding. *The Life of Joseph F. Smith.* Salt Lake City: Deseret News Press, 1938.

Smith, William, ed. *A Dictionary of the Bible.* Philadelphia: The John C. Winston Company, 1948.

Sparks, H. F. D. *The Apocryphal Old Testament.* Oxford: Claredon Press, 1984.

Staniforth, Maxwell, trans. *Early Christian Writings—The Apostolic Fathers.* New York: Dorset Press, 1986.

Thayer, Joseph Henry, D. D. *The New Thayer's Greek-English Lexicon of the New Testament.* Massachusetts: Hendrickson Publisher, 1981.

Vine, W. E., *An Expository Dictionary of New Testament Words.* Old Tappan, New Jersey: Fleming H. Revell Co., 1966.

Webster, Noah. *Noah Webster's First Edition of an American Dictionary of the English Language.* Anaheim, California: The Foundation for American Christian Education, 1967.

Whitney, Orson F. *The Life of Heber C. Kimball.* 3rd ed. Salt Lake City: Bookcraft, 1967.

Wilson, William. *Old Testament Word Studies.* Grand Rapids, Michigan: Kregel Publications, 1978.

Woodruff, Wilford. *The Discourses of Wilford Woodruff.* G. Homer Durham, ed. Salt Lake City: Bookcraft, 1969.

Young, Brigham. *Manuscript History of Brigham Young, 1846–1847.* Elden J. Watson, ed. 1971.

Subject Index

— A —

Aaron (brother of Moses), 5, 36
Aaronic Priesthood, 6, 95
  restoration of, 34, 41, 42, 58, 65, 80, 135, 136, 152
Abraham, 5, 34, 78, 93, 95, 146, 147, 177
  book of, 33, 148
  descendants of, 33
  father of, 74
  ordained by Melchizedek, 35
  promises to, 36, 43
  vision of, 31, 33, 136
  visit of angels to, 60
Accountability, 157
Acts of Uzziah, 148
Adam, 5, 29, 32, 95, 97, 136, 141, 142, 145, 146
  book of the generations of, 148
  Enoch ordained by, 35
  keys received by, 35
  prophecies of, 91–92, 153
  taught by angels, 60
Adamic language, 124
Adam-ondi-Ahman, 92, 153
Admonitions, 132
Adversary. *See* Satan
Age of Reason, The (pamphlet), 106–7
Akkadian language, 5
Alexander the Great, 48
Alma the Younger, on angels, 62, 99
  on brass plates, 146
  on feelings, 168
  on heed and diligence, 134
  on revelation, 4–5
  on scriptures, 185
  rebellion of, 74
Ammon, on seers, 8–9
Amos, 5, 130
  on prophets, 19, 26
Angel, appearance to Cornelius, 133
  appearance to Hagar, 75
  appearance to King Benjamin, 133
  apearance to Nephi, 128
Angels, 80, 176
  ministering of, 95, 99
  ministry of, 60–66, 181–82
Anointing, 134
Anti-Mormon literature, 122
Apocalypse of Abraham, 33
Apocryphal writings, 26, 32, 33, 149, 150
Apostasy, described through metaphor of adultery, 172
  following meridian, 10, 29, 185
  Jewish, 48–50
  of Israel, 6, 130
Apostle, meaning of word, 21, 47
Apostles, 11, 24, 38
  meridian, 3, 15, 21, 23, 24, 45, 74
Arabic language, 5
Asaph (Hebrew form of Joseph), 58
Ashteroth, priests of, 158–59
Assumption of Moses, 149
Assuredness, 168
Atonement, 143
Authority, 14, 16, 19, 34–42, 81, 180, 187
  necessity of, 23
  of Apostles, 21
  restoration of, 137

— B —

Baal, priests of, 158–59
Babel, tower of, 118
Balaam, 5, 83
Baptism, 39, 52–53, 87, 116, 135, 136
  covenant of, 180–81
  necessity of, 13
  practiced among Jews, 67
Behemoth, 139
Benjamin (Nephite prophet-king), people of, 165
  visit of angel to, 133
Bethlehem, 78
Bible, 12, 14, 15, 16–17, 19, 24, 34, 113, 122, 127, 129, 138, 187
  brass plates more extensive than, 146–47
  German, 53–54

Joseph Smith Translation, 28–29, 37, 60, 63–64, 127, 128, 137–38, 152
  not complete, 128
  not replaced by Book of Mormon, 79
  prophecies of Restoration, 55–56
  tests for discerning prophets, 70
  understanding through Holy Ghost, 114
Book of Abraham, 33, 148
Book of the acts of Solomon, 148
Book of Enoch, 148
Book of Gad, 148
Book of the generations of Adam, 148
Book of Jasher, 148
Book of Maccabees, 48–49
Book of Mormon, 127, 128, 130, 138, 146, 179
  function of prophets of, 8–9
  not a replacement for Bible, 79
  sealed portion, 142–43
  source of gospel knowledge, 17
  stick of Ephraim, 60
  translation of, 23, 137, 152
Book of Moses, 31
Book of Nathan the prophet, 148
Book of Revelation, 66
Book of Samuel the seer, 148
Book of Shemaiah, 148
Book of the wars of the Lord, 148
Brass plates of Laban, 60, 144–47
Brother of Jared, 136
Bullock, Thomas, 54

— C —

Caiaphas, 105
Cainan (land of), 32
Cainan (Old Testament prophet), 148
Caleb, 148
Catholics, 40
Celestial kingdom, 41
Charisma, 72
Charity, 160, 172
Children, 132, 181–82
Christianity, 10, 18, 70–72, 105–6
Christians, 106
Christ. *See* Jesus Christ
Christs, false, 69, 155
Church, governed by spirit of prophecy, 129–31
  one true, 159
  prophets the constitution of, 16
  true and living, 13–14
Church members, ability and responsibility to be prophets, 90

Comforter, 132–33, 184
  See also Holy Ghost
Common Sense (pamphlet), 106
Contrite spirit, 86
Converts, 70–71
Cornelius, 133
Council in heaven, 22, 25, 26, 29–36, 37, 41–46, 54, 162
Counsel of the Lord, 25–27, 29
Covenant, gospel, 179–80
  of baptism, 180–81
Covenant relationship with God, 171
Covenants, 44, 85, 136–37, 171–74
Cowdery, Oliver, 137–38, 149
  baptism of, 136
  on receiving Aaronic Priesthood, 165
  on room of plates in Hill Cumorah, 144–45
  peace spoken to, 165
  priesthood restored to, 29, 44, 65, 80, 135
Creation, 33, 35, 143, 146
Cultists, 86
Cults, characteristics of, 70–72
Cumorah, 144

— D —

Daniel, 5
David, 78
Dead Sea Scrolls, 57, 59
Degrees of glory, 37, 40–41, 108, 135, 143
Devils, 87, 88, 109, 113
  See also Satan
Didache, 77
Diligence, 134, 174
Discernment, divine pattern of, 85–88
  power of, 163
  tests of, 109–10
Dispensation of the fulness of times, 31, 150–51, 187
Doctrine, false, 12, 85, 155, 160
  restoration of, 24, 107
Doctrines of salvation, 12, 17, 110
Dogma of sufficiency, 122, 125
Dreams, 34

— E —

Earth, paradisiacal glory of, 186
  restoration to pristine state, 185–86
  transfiguration of, 149
Ecumenism, 158–60
Eden, Garden of, 136, 182

Subject Index

Edification, 133
Egyptian religion, symbolism of, 125
Eliab, 72–73, 78
Elias, 34, 41, 51, 53, 64, 65, 152
Elihu, 148
Elijah, 3, 41, 42, 50–53, 58, 65, 126, 127, 130
  contest with priests of Baal, 158–59
  keys restored by, 34, 152
Elisabeth (mother of John the Baptist), 142, 182
Elisha, 3, 130
Endowment, 44, 188
Enlightenment, 166
Enoch, 25, 36, 73, 76, 97, 136
  book of, 148
  calling of, 31–33, 45
  city of, 183
  priesthood held by, 93
  prophecy of, 61
  taught by angels, 60
  vision of, 35, 112
  writings of, 149, 153
Enos (Nephite prophet), 25
Enos (Old Testament prophet), 148
Ephraim, 56
Equality, 84–85, 115, 157, 163–64, 187–88
Esaias, 148, 153
Essenes, prophet anticipated by, 57–58
Eternal life, 117
  See also Exaltation; Salvation
Ether, gold plates of, 144, 145
Eve, 142, 146
  prophetess, 91–92, 182
Evil spirits, 85–87, 177–78
Exaltation, 21, 101, 110, 132, 177
  See also Eternal life; Salvation
Exhortation, 132
Ezekiel, 5, 40, 128
  visions of, 27–28, 29, 33, 96
Ezias, 148
Ezra, 129

— F —

Faith, 14, 112, 129, 131, 136, 151–52, 156, 187, 188
  signs through, 160
  through prophecy, 115, 118
Fall of Adam, 143, 182
False Christs, 12, 69, 155
False doctrines, 12, 85, 155, 160
False prophets, 7, 12, 25, 54, 69–70, 79, 85, 87–88, 155

False revelations, 155
False spirits, 83, 85
False traditions, 147
Falsehood, 155
Fear, 165
Feelings, 167–68
Fidelity, 172
Fielding, Joseph, on peace, 164
First Vision, 17, 34, 39, 55–56, 135, 164
Foreordination, 22–23, 25, 33, 41, 44, 55

— G —

Gabriel, 165
Gad, book of, 148
Garden of Eden, 136, 182
Gathering of Israel. *See* Israel, gathering of
Genealogy, traced by Lehi, 146
Genesis, book of, 127
Gentiles, 49, 64
German Bible, 53–54
Gideon, 165
Gift of the Holy Ghost. *See* Holy Ghost, gift of
Gift of prophecy, had by women, 181–83
Gift of tongues, 97–98
Gifts of the Spirit, 97–98, 181–82
Ginosko, 172
God, 153, 166, 178
  Christ introduced by, 38–39
  foreknowledge of, 23
  help from, 131–32
  justice of, 11, 15, 70, 156–57
  knowledge of, 11, 163–64, 171–74
  nature of, 179
  no respecter of persons, 84–85, 107, 121
  not author of confusion, 159
  omnipotence of, 156
  power and authority given to prophets, 8
  priesthood the authority of, 14
  prophets chosen by, 4, 16
  surrender to, 160
  wisdom of, 16
Godhead, 80
Godliness, attributes of, 172, 173, 178
Gold plates, 144–45
Gospel, covenant of, 179–80
  teaching of, 11–13
Gospel of John, 127
Grammatical errors, 124

Grand Council of heaven. *See* Council in heaven
Greek language, 114
Greek thought, 173
Greek tradition, 174
Greek words, *ginosko*, 172
  parakaleo, 133
  paraklesis, 133
  parakletos, 133
  prophetes, 7
Greeks, 79

— H —

Hagar, 75
Haggai, 5, 25, 130
Haran, 136
Harmony, 166–67
Hatch, Edwin, *The Influence of Greek Ideas on Christianity*, 10
  on modern Christianity, 10
Hawaii, 73
Hawaii (book), 86
Heavenly council. *See* Council in heaven
Hebrew language, 114
Hebrew prophecy, metaphor of adultery in, 172
Hebrew words, *hozen*, 6
  nabi, 5, 7, 20
  ro'eh, 6
  sod, 26
  yada, 171
Hell, 143
Herod Antipas, 51
Hezekiah, 78
Hill Cumorah, 144
History, 15
Holy Ghost, 107, 118, 136
  characteristics of, 163
  comforter, 132–33, 184
  gift of, 87, 90, 99–100, 116–17, 134, 137, 180, 181
  given to Adam, 91–92
  importance of, 100
  language of, 114
  peace through, 164
  preaching by power of, 184–85
  revelation from, 12, 71–72, 169, 183
  speaking by, 9–10, 163, 182
  teaching by, 111
Holy Spirit of promise, 118
Horeb, 28
Hosea, 25, 74, 130
Hozen, 6
Hypocrites, 85

— I —

Idolatry, 159
Ignorance, 12, 153, 160, 177
Influence of Greek Ideas on Christianity, The (book), 10
Intolerance, of prophets, 157
Isaac, 146, 147, 177
Isaiah, 5, 40, 52, 63–64, 75, 78, 124, 130
  on joy, 164
  prophecies of, 55, 63–64, 72
  visions of, 27, 29, 33, 96
Israel, apostasy of, 6
  Babylonian captivity, 51
  children of, 28–29, 94–95
  gathering of, 27, 29, 55, 64, 66, 128, 151, 154–55
  lost tribes of, 58, 147
  modern nation of, 153–54
  promised lands to be inherited by, 141
Ivins, Anthony W., on function of prophets, 9

— J —

Jackson County, Missouri, temple to be built in, 152–53
Jacob (Old Testament prophet), 59, 136, 147, 177
Jacob's ladder, 37
Jacob (son of Lehi), on faith, 115
James, on asking of God, 135
  on being doers of the word, 132
  on belief of devils, 113
  on impartiality of God, 121
  on wisdom from above, 166
Jared, 148
Jasher, book of, 148
Jehovah, 123
  See also Jesus Christ
Jeremiah, 5, 10, 32, 40, 73, 145, 146
  calling of, 28, 33
  on prophets standing in counsel of the Lord, 25, 26, 30
  on word of God, 167
  prophecy of, 55
  tradition about return of, 51
Jeremy, 148
Jerusalem, 145
  temple at, 49, 183
  temple to be built at, 152
Jesse, 78

Subject Index

Jesus Christ, 4, 12, 50–51, 53, 66, 74, 113, 118, 148, 159, 171
  advancement from grace to grace, 122, 149
  Apostles, 21, 74, 76–77
  appearance, after resurrection, 165
  atonement, 143
  at place of purification, 150
  baptism of, 38–39, 179
  Church of, 70–72, 105, 130
  comforter, 132–33
  conversation with Samaritan woman, 57
  example, 13, 45–46, 84, 162
  high mountain experience of, 37
  instructions to Apostles, 38, 39, 45
  introduced by the Father, 38–39
  Jews to know of, 146–47
  lack of formal training, 74
  Last Supper, 71, 96
  law of Moses fulfilled by, 79
  light of, 157
  ministry, 138
  miracle of loaves and fishes, 22
  Nephite ministry, 39, 144
  not recognized by Jews, 114, 127
  on feeling spirit of revelation, 167–68
  on Godhead, 80
  on John the Baptist, 116
  on knowledge, 173, 179–80
  on peace, 164
  on restoration of the earth, 186
  on spiritual equality, 85
  on truth, 174–75, 179–80
  physical appearance of, 72
  priesthood of, 14
  prophets respected by, 3–4
  rejection of, 74, 122
  return heralded by angels, 61–66
  on road to Emmaus, 167
  rule during Millennium, 58
  salvation through, 160
  second comforter promised by, 96
  second coming, 61–67, 143
  selflessness of, 163
  sent of his Father, 37–38, 77
  Sermon on the Mount, 19, 71, 123
  special witnesses of, 116
  submissiveness of, 161–62
  taking name of, 102, 181
  testimony had by lost tribes, 147
  transfiguration, 136
  types of, 101–2
  witnesses of, 180–81, 183
Jethro, 29, 36, 45, 148

Jews, 40, 60, 106, 129, 146–47
  apostasy of, 48–50
  Christ rejected by, 114, 127
  tradition of Messiah ben Joseph, 56, 58–60
  traditions of, 67
Jihad, 186
Job, 139
Joel, 25
John the Baptist, 5, 22, 36, 38, 50–54, 62–65, 72, 116
  Aaronic Priesthood restored by, 34, 42, 58, 65, 80, 135
  record to be revealed, 149
John the Revelator, 7, 18, 66
  Gospel of, 127
  on Christ's return to Mount Zion, 61
  on exaltation, 101
  on prophets, 74–75
  on teaching, 84
  on truth, 174–75
  parchment hidden up by, 149
  visions of, 37, 96
Jonah, 5, 25
Joseph of Egypt, 58–60, 146
  patriarchal blessing of, 59
  prophecy of, 55
  stick of, 59
  writings of, 148
Joshua, 95
  on choosing whom to serve, 158
Joy, 164–65
Judah, restoration to Palestine, 58
  scattering and gathering of, 27
  stick of, 59, 147
  See also Israel, gathering of
Judas Iscariot, 83
Jude, 148–49
Judgment day, 108, 156–57
Justice, of God, 11, 15, 70, 156–57

— K —

Keys, 45, 123, 180
  of gathering of Israel, 29
  restoration of, 34, 54, 80–81, 100, 137, 152
Kimball, Heber C., mision to British Isles, 73–74
Kindness, 160, 172
Kingdoms of glory. *See* Degrees of glory
Kirtland Temple, 41

Knowledge, 91, 109, 142, 152, 171–74, 177, 179
　equality of, 115, 163–64
Koran, 106

— L —

Laman and Lemuel, 168
Languages, knowledge of ancient, 114
　limitations of, 124–28
Last Supper, 71, 96
Laub, George, on Joseph Smith, 54
Law of Moses, 18, 60–61, 70, 79, 123, 129
　fulfilled by Christ, 79
Law of witnesses, 11–12, 34–35, 79–81
Laws, spiritual, 81–85, 88
Laying on of hands, 81
Lectures on Faith, 91
Lehi, brass plates brought by, 60, 145–46
　on unchanging nature of the Spirit, 128
　vision of, 98
Leviathan, 124, 139
Liahona, 145
Light of Christ, 157
Long-suffering, 160
Lost scriptures, to be restored, 141–54
Lost tribes of Israel. *See* Israel, lost tribes of
Lot, 60
Love, 132, 172
Loyalty, 163
Lucifer. *See* Satan
Luke, 183
　on daughters of Philip, 183
　on other writings, 149

— M —

Maccabeans, 49, 57
Maccabees, book of, 48–49
McConkie, Bruce R., on exaltation, 101
　on incompleteness of scriptures, 128–29
　on meaning of scriptures, 184
　on scripture study, 135
　on sealed portion of Book of Mormon, 143
　on testimony, 185
　on translation of scriptures, 127–28
Mahalaleel, 148
Malachi, 51, 64, 65, 124–25, 126, 127, 130

Manasseh, 146
Manifestations, 25, 160
Manual of Discipline, 58
Manoah, 75
Mark, 183
Marriage, 172
　eternal, 34, 118
Mary (mother of Jesus), 182, 183
Masoretic text, 126
Matthias, 3
Melchizedek (Old Testament prophet), 35–36, 97, 116, 148
Melchizedek Priesthood, 6, 23, 25, 93–94
　received by Moses, 29
　restoration of, 34, 41, 42, 80, 99–101, 137, 142, 173
　taken from Israel, 76, 94–95
Meridian Church, 71, 101, 105, 118, 183
Meridian dispensation, 81
Meridian prophets, understood through modern prophets, 114
Meridian Saints, 6, 7–8, 15
Mesopotamian texts, "heavenly council theme" in, 30
Messiah ben David, 58
Messiah ben Joseph, 56, 58–60
Methuselah, 35, 148
Micah, 25, 130
Michael, 32
Michener, James, *Hawaii*, 86
Millennium, 58, 141
Ministering of angels, 95, 99
Ministry of angels, 60–66, 181–82
Miracle of loaves and fishes, 22
Miracles, 14
Missionaries, 24, 38, 70–71, 162
Moriah, 136
Mormon, 128, 138
　Book of Mormon abridged by, 144
　on ministering of angels, 99
　on receiving greater things, 143
　on words of Christ, 144
　warnings of, 119
Mormonism, accused of being a cult, 70
　accused of narrow-mindedness, 159–60
Moroni, 138
　appearance to Joseph Smith, 126, 127, 165
　Book of Ether abridged by, 144
　on Book of Mormon, 179
　on his imperfections, 78

Subject Index

on knowing truth of all things, 163
on sealed portion of Book of Mormon, 143
Moses, 3, 7, 32, 40, 50, 52, 55, 70, 73, 74, 76, 78–79, 83, 100, 121, 122, 127, 129, 136
   appearance on Mount of Transfiguration, 53
   blessing to tribe of Joseph, 59
   book of, 31, 127
   calling of, 33, 45
   illustration using eagles, 124
   keys of gathering of Israel held by, 29, 34, 41, 42, 152
   on prophets, 7, 102
   ordination of, 36
   priesthood received by, 29
   taken from children of Israel, 76, 94–95
   type of Christ, 101–2
   visions of, 28, 31, 112–13
   See also Law of Moses
Mosiah, sons of, 74
Mount Carmel, 158
Mount of Transfiguration, 29, 53, 65, 80, 136, 149
Mount Pisgah, 51
Mount Shelem, 136
Mount Simeon, 136
Mount Sinai, 28–29, 36, 45, 94, 123, 129, 136
Mountains, 28, 29, 31–32, 37
Muslims, 40
Mysteries of God, 134
Mysteries of heaven, 151
Mysteries of the kingdom, 93, 96, 108, 137

— N —

Nabi, 5, 7, 20
Nathan, 5, 78
   book of, 148
Nauvoo Temple, 41
Nephi, 138, 168
   instructions of angel to, 128
   on Holy Ghost, 90–91
   on prophecies of Joseph of Egypt, 148
   on putting trust in man, 163
   on scriptures in last days, 147
   on sealed portion of Book of Mormon, 142–43
   plates of, 144
   testimony of, 174

vision of, 98–99
Nephites, 130
   ministry of Christ to, 39, 144
   righteous society of, 183
Neum, 148
New Cults, The (book), 70
New Testament, 129, 172
   calling of prophets of, 37–40
   function of prophets in, 7–8
   lost books of, 149–50
   Old Testament understood through, 113–14
Nicene Creed, 19
Noah (Old Testament prophet), 148
   ordination of, 35

— O —

Obedience, 12, 87, 88, 112, 161, 166, 174, 187, 188
Old Testament, 128, 129–30, 138, 171–72
   apocryphal texts, 26, 32, 33
   calling of prophets of, 25–36
   function of prophets in, 5–6
   lost books of, 147–49
   New Testament understood through, 113–14
   pure version on brass plates, 146–47
   washing and anointing in, 134
Opposition, 117, 155
Ordinance, synonym for law or statute, 87
Ordinances, 14, 19, 22, 24, 82
   authority needed for, 18
   baptism, 180
   had by lost tribes, 147
   power of godliness manifest in, 137
   restoration of, 107
   temple, 101
Ordinations, 7, 81, 87
   of prophets, 35–36
   premortal, 31

— P —

Pagan symbolism, 124–25
Paine, Thomas, *The Age of Reason*, 106–7
   Common Sense, 106
   on revelation, 106–7
Palestine, 48
   restoration of Judah to, 58
Paradise, 143
Parakaleo, 133

Paraklesis, 133
Parakletos, 133
Parents, 132
Patience, 160, 172
Patriarchal blessings, 126, 132, 183
Paul, 7, 10, 18, 71, 73, 74, 76, 79, 168, 173, 183
  caught up to third heaven, 37
  lost epistles of, 149–50
  on apostles, 38
  on assurance, 168
  on the gospel, 22
  on heirs of God, 188
  on kingdom of God, 169
  on latter days, 10
  on law of Moses, 61
  on more sure word of prophecy, 117
  on need of men and women for each other, 177, 183
  on prophets, 16, 82
  on restoration, 150–51
  on revelation, 166
  on spiritual blessings, 44
  on spiritual gifts, 97–98
  on things of God, 11, 112
  pagan symbolism used by, 125
  visions of, 96
  warnings of, 119
Peace, 97, 164–65
Peniel, 136
Persecution, 117
Peter, 39, 53, 66, 71, 83, 172
  on speaking by Holy Ghost, 10
Peter, James, and John, 40
  keys received by, 29, 80
  Melchizedek Priesthood restored by, 34, 44, 80
  on Mount of Transfiguration, 37, 53, 136, 149, 178
Pharisees, 80
Philip, daughters of, 183
Pilate, Pontius, 180
Plan of salvation, 11, 12, 168, 173, 187
Power, 24, 115, 118
Preaching, 9–10
Premortal life, 22–33, 41, 143
Priestcraft, 10, 77
Priesthood, 13, 18, 24, 187, 188
  Aaronic, 6, 34, 41, 42, 95
  conferred by laying on of hands, 81
  granted to every worthy male, 90
  held by lost tribes, 147
  keys of, 54, 123, 180
  Melchizedek, 6, 23, 25, 29, 34, 41, 42, 93, 94–95, 99–101

ordinations, 87
power of, 93–94, 117
prophets necessary to, 14–15
restoration of, 34, 41, 42, 58, 65, 80–81, 99–101, 107, 135–37, 141–42, 151, 152, 173
Prophecy, all may receive spirit of, 181–87
  discernment of, 155–69
  gift of, 182–83
  individual, 116–17
  more sure word of, 117–18
  need for, 105–19
  See also Spirit of prophecy
Prophetes, 7
Prophetesses, 7, 91–92, 182–83
Prophetic guilds, 6
Prophets, calling of, 11, 21–46
  Church members to be, 90–102
  constitution of the Church, 16
  discerning of, 69–88
  essential to Restoration, 67
  examples, 188
  false, 7, 12, 25, 54, 69–70, 79, 85, 87–88, 155
  foreordination of, 22–23, 25
  function of, 4–10
  intolerance of, 157
  meaning of word, 5
  need for, 3–19
  of lost tribes, 147
  presiding, 6
  profile of, 75–81
  pure motives of, 76–77
  revelators, 77
  righteousness of, 75–76
  teaching a primary function of, 116
  unity among, 82
Protestants, 40
Pseudepigraphic works, 149
Ptolemy, 48
Purity, 166

— R —

Radio ministries, 111
Rebellion, 168
Religion, characteristics of true, 155–63
Repentance, 13, 15
Restitution of all things, 150–53
Restoration, 34, 48, 55–67, 107, 128, 138, 141, 173
  doctrinal, 150–53
  of all things, 185–86
  prophecies of, 55–56

Subject Index

traditions of, 56–60
See also Priesthood, restoration of
Resurrection, 64
Revelation, 14, 17, 22–24, 81, 91, 106–7, 110, 113–14, 130–31, 139
  assurance of, given to Apostles, 22
  book of, 66
  enlightenment through, 166
  false, 155
  gospel acquired by, 12–13
  harmony of, 166–67
  language limitations of, 124–28
  myths concerning, 122–28
  personal, 108–9, 116–17, 126, 168
  See also Spirit of revelation
Reverence, 135
Rigdon, Sidney, 40, 42, 83
Righteousness, 12, 112, 113–34, 169, 172
  meaning of, 178–79
Ro'eh, 6
Robinson, Stephen E., on apostasy of Jews, 49

— S —

Sacrament, 181
Sacred Grove, 135
Sacrifice, 112, 172, 188
Salvation, 101–2, 160–61, 175, 177, 178
  See also Eternal life; Exaltation
Samaritan tradition, of prophet of restoration, 56–57
Samuel (Old Testament prophet), 72–73
  David anointed by, 78
Samuel the seer, book of, 148
Sanhedrin, 105
Satan, 15, 54, 69, 84, 85, 87, 113, 124, 155, 164
Science, 156
Scriptures, 12, 113, 123
  additional, 70–71
  ambiguity of, 125–26
  Church not directed by, 129–31
  meaning of, 184
  not complete, 128
  of lost tribes, 147
  original manuscripts of, 125
  study of, 126, 134–35
  to be restored, 141–54
Sealing power, 18
Second comforter, 96
Second Coming, 61–67, 143
Secret lines of authority, 86

Secrets of Enoch, 32
Seers, 6, 8–9, 25
Seleucus, 48
Selflessness, 163–64
Self-reliance, 168–69
Semitic tradition, 174
Septuagint, 72, 126
Sermon on the Mount, 19, 71, 123
Service, 175
Seth, 148
Seventy elders of Israel, 95
Sexual immorality, 86
Shem, 148
Shemaiah, book of, 148
Shepherds, 183
Sign seeking, 135, 160
Simeon, 183
Simeon, Mount, 32, 136
Sinai, Mount, 28–29, 36, 45, 94, 123, 129, 136
Sincerity, 12
Sins, remission of, 181
Smith, George A., on happiness, 164
Smith, Hyrum, 119
  foreordination of, 44
Smith, Joseph, 18, 31, 32, 62, 70, 73, 79, 83, 149, 167, 174, 181
  appearance of Moroni to, 165
  appearance to Brigham Young, 165
  authority received by, 34–35
  Bible translation, 28–29, 37, 60, 63–64, 127, 128, 137–38, 152
  Book of Mormon translated by, 23
  calling as prophet, 40–43, 46
  First Vision, 17, 34, 39, 55–56, 135, 164
  foreordination, 41
  instructed by Moroni, 126
  James read by, 135
  keys received by, 29
  on assurance of eternal life, 117
  on authority, 23, 34
  on constitution of the kingdom of God, 16
  on faith, 136, 151–52, 177
  on false prophets, 69
  on foreordination, 22–23, 25, 44
  on Grand Council, 33
  on his baptism, 136
  on Holy Ghost given to Adam, 91
  on joy, 164, 165
  on justice of God, 156
  on knowledge, 115, 134, 177
  on more sure word of prophecy, 117
  on priesthood, of Adam, 35

on prophets, 25, 77
on pure intelligence, 166
on receiving Holy Ghost, 137–38
on revelation, 91, 121
on reverence, 135
on righteousness, 134, 179
on second comforter, 96
on spirit of prophecy, 18–19
on tasting principle of eternal life, 168
only a portion of gold plates translated by, 142
plates received by, 144–45
priesthood restored to, 58, 65, 80, 135
privilege of translation lost by, 24
rejection of, 122
restoration through, 152, 186
revelations to, 93, 160, 162
source of gospel knowledge, 17
"that prophet," 48–54
visions of, 25, 40–41, 108, 134
Smith, Joseph F., mission to Hawaii, 73
on God not suffering head of Church to transgress, 83
on prophets, 83–84
on revival era, 87
vision of the redemption of the dead, 44, 135
Smith, Mary Fielding, 182
Snow, Eliza R., 182
Solomon, book of the acts of, 148
Sons of Levi, 64–65
Spirit of prophecy, 7, 18–19, 82, 97–98, 107, 110, 114–18, 163, 171
Church directed by, 129–31
functions of, 131–33
requisites to, 133–37
truths fundamental to, 128–31
voice of warning, 132
Spirit of prophecy and revelation, 9, 14–15, 16, 105, 111, 113, 116, 118, 130, 133, 135, 136, 162, 169, 180, 187
extended to all who properly seek it, 185
heirs of, 181–84
source of doctrine, 110
Spirit of revelation, 10, 14, 16, 71, 100, 114, 122–23, 152, 165, 166, 167, 178
branches and fruits of, 184–85
characteristics of, 163–69
needed to teach, 110–11
Spirit world, 41, 63, 143, 156
missionary work in, 64

Spirits, false, 83, 85
Spiritual gifts, 97–98, 181–82
Spiritual laws, 81–85, 88
Stephen, testimony of, 60–61
Stick of Judah, 147
Submissiveness, 162–63
Supernatural experiences, salvation not obtained through, 160
Sword of Laban, 145
Symbolism, pagan, 124–25
Syria, 48

— T —

Taheb, 56–57
Talmud, 59
Targumming, 129
Taylor, John, 16
foreordination of, 44
"Teacher of Righteousness," 58
Teaching, 118
by Holy Ghost, 111
primary form of prophecy, 116
Television ministries, 111
Temple, in Jackson County, Missouri, 152–53
in Jerusalem, 152
Temple ordinances, 101, 143
Temple worship, restoration of, 58–59
Temples, 24, 28, 44, 67, 136, 152, 184
Terah, 74
Testimony, bearing of, 181
Tolerance, 160
Tongues, gift of, 97–98
Tradition, 19
Transfiguration, of the earth, 149
of Moses, 112–13
See also Mount of Transfiguration
Translated beings, 143
Translation, of scriptures, 126–27, 137–38
Trustworthiness, 163, 174
Truth, 9, 12, 111, 113, 155, 159, 166, 169, 179
gospel definition of, 174–80
perversion of, 111
Turks, religion of, 106
Types, of Christ, 101–2

— U —

United States, Constitution, 131
Urim and Thummim, 149
Uzziah, acts of, 148

— V —

Virtue, 166, 172
Vision of degrees of glory, 40–41, 108
  See also Degrees of glory
Vision of the redemption of the dead, 44, 135
Visions, 25–49, 96, 108–9, 112, 134

— W —

Warmth, 167
Warnings, 132
Washing, 134
Whitmer, David, 145
Wisdom, 165
Witnesses, law of, 11–12, 34–35, 79–81
  of Christ, 180–81
Women, 181–83, 187
Woodruff, Wilford, description of Brigham Young and Heber C. Kimball, 73
  foreordination of, 44
  on being witnesses of Christ, 181
  on president of Church not leading people astray, 83
  on work of the Lord, 44–45

— Y —

Yada, 171
Young, Brigham, appearance of Joseph Smith to, 165
  foreordination of, 44
  mission to British Isles, 73
  on room full of plates in Hill Cumorah, 144–45
  on wording of scriptures, 126–27

— Z —

Zacharias, 142, 165
Zadokites, 57
Zechariah, 5, 25, 130
Zedekiah, 146
Zenock, 148
Zenos, 148
Zephaniah, 25

Scripture Index

OLD TESTAMENT

Genesis
  5:21–24   32
  14:26–33 (JST)   36
  14:30–32 (JST)   93
  16:12 (NEB)   75
  18:2   60
  19:1 (JST)   60
  20:7   5
  49:22–26   59
  50:24–33 (JST)   55
  50:24–38 (JST)   60
  50:27, 33 (JST)   48

Exodus
  3:1   28
  3:2   28
  3:2 (JST)   47
  3:5   28
  3:10   47
  3:10, 12, 13–15   29
  3:11   76
  3:12   30
  4:14–15   73
  4:27   28
  7:1   5
  15:17   28
  18:5   28
  19:5–6, 10–11   94
  19:11   121
  34:1–2 (JST)   95
  34:27   129

Numbers
  11:24–29   95
  11:29   7, 90
  21:14   148

Deuteronomy
  3:21–22, 28   6
  13:2–3   173
  17:6   81
  18:15   101
  18:18   50, 57
  18:22   5

  19:15   81
  32:11   124
  33:13–17   59
  34:9   6

Joshua
  24:14–25   158

Judges
  6:24   165
  13:22–23   75

1 Samuel
  9:9   6
  10:5   6
  16:7   73
  19:20   6

2 Samuel
  1:18   148
  7:3–16   78

1 Kings
  11:41   148
  18:17–40   159
  19:1   159
  20:35   6

2 Kings
  1:8   6
  2:3, 5, 7, 15   6
  2:9–15   6
  4:1, 38   6
  5:22   6
  6:1   6
  9:1   6

1 Chronicles
  29:29   148

2 Chronicles
  9:29   148
  12:15   148
  26:22   27, 148

Nehemiah		2:20–37	172
8:8	129	6:27 (RSV)	6
		20:9	167
Job		22:15–16	173
40:15–24	139	23:17	10
41:1–10	124	23:18, 21–22	26
		23:18, 22	25
Psalms		30:21	55
7:14	124		
19:7–11	169	**Ezekiel**	
78:54	28	1:26–28	28
104:25–27	124	2:1–5	28
		2:6	30
Isaiah		2:6–8	28
1:1	27	2:9–10	28
6:5	27	3:1–3	28
6:5–6	75		
6:7	27	**Hosea**	
6:8	27	1:2	74
6:9–10 (JST)	27	4:1–2	173
6:11–13	27	9:8	6
14:1–23	124		
27:1	139	**Amos**	
35:10	164	3:7	3, 6, 19, 26
38:1–5	78		
40:3–5	52	**Haggai**	
40:4–5	63	1:13	6
41:22	5	2:1	5
43:9	5		
49:1–11	55	**Zechariah**	
52:1–2	141	1:7	5
52:10	61	13:4	6
53:2	72		
53:3	72	**Malachi**	
55:12	164	3:1	48, 52
		4:1	65
Jeremiah		4:2	125
1:4–5	28	4:5	65
1:6	73	4:5–6	51, 139
1:6–10	28		

NEW TESTAMENT

Matthew		10:8	71
1:22	155	10:41	69, 85
1:25	172	11:10	64
3:4	72	13:15	167
3:17	39	14:2	51
3:25 (JST)	84	15:8–9	159
4:8 (JST)	37, 45	15:13	186
7:14	72	16:6	159
7:15	7, 69	16:13–14	51
9:18–24 (JST)	68	16:19	21, 123
10:1–6	71	17:1–9	37

17:1–11	80	7:16–17	173
17:3–4	65	7:16–18	77
17:10–14 (JST)	53	7:17	173
23:8–12	85	7:28	38
24:11	7	7:40–41	52
24:14	53	8:13	80
24:31	61	8:16–18	80
24:32 (JST)	119	8:30–32	180
28:19–20	39	9:4 (RSV)	38
		9:4	161
Mark		10:37	161
1:2	64	12:44	38
1:13	45	13:20	38
7:6	8	14:6	72, 159, 175
14:36	162		
16:14–20	71	14:7	173
		14:9	46
Luke		14:12	4
1:1	149	14:16–23	96
1:12	165	14:23	118
1:13	165	14:26	96
1:46–55	182	14:27	164
1:67	8	15:16	21, 77
1:76	63	16:18–19	40
2:8–17	62	15:26	22
2:10	164	16:7–13	22
2:25–35	183	16:12–14	72
3:4–11 (JST)	52, 64	17:3	172
3:10 (JST)	151	18:37	180
6:13	21	20:13	21
6:26	39	20:21	38
7:39	8	21:18–19	39
9:19	51		
10:4	71	Acts	
22:35–36	71	1:6–7	151
24:32	167	2:16–18	7
24:36	165	3:21	67, 141
24:37	165	7:52–53	60
24:49	45	10:4	133
		10:44–47	8
John		11:28	8
1:19–21	50	14:14–15	78
1:22–23	52	14:15 (NEB)	4
3:20–21	174	17:28	125
4:18–19	8	21:8–9	183
4:25	57	21:10	8
4:34	37		
5:19	161	Romans	
5:25–29	156	8:16–17	188
5:30	38, 161	14:17	169
5:41	163		
6:38	38, 161	1 Corinthians	
7:5	74	1:21	173
7:15	74	2:1	10
7:16	38, 161	2:3–4	73

2:9	173	Hebrews	
2:11	11	1:1–2	121
2:11–14	112	1:9	164
5:9	150	3:1	38, 45
9:14	76	4:15	4
9:18	71	5:10	45
11:4–5	8		
11:11	177, 183	James	
12:28–29	7	1:22	132
14:1	97	2:19	113
14:3	8	3:17	121, 155, 166
14:3, 31	8		
14:29–31	6	5:17	78
14:29–32	7	5:17 (NEB)	4
14:31	171		
14:31–32	82	1 Peter	
14:32	16	3:18–20	156
		4:6	156
2 Corinthians			
4:7	4	2 Peter	
11:7	71	1:5–8	172
12:2–3	37	1:19	117
		1:21	10
Galatians		2:1	7
3:19	61		
3:19 (JST)	61	1 John	
		1:5–6	174
Ephesians		2:27	84
1:3–4	44	4:1	7, 70
1:10	151	4:5–6	75
1:18	166		
2:19–20	7	Jude	
4:11	7	1:14–15	61
4:17–19	168	1:9, 14–15	149
Philippians		Revelation	
2:12	157	1:5–6	101
		4:1–4	37
1 Thessalonians		5:9–10	101
1:5	22, 168	7:4	68
5:19–20	119	10:11	66
		13:8	45
1 Timothy		14:1	61
2:7	38	14:6–7	62
		19:10	7, 105
2 Timothy		21:5	162
4:3	10		

BOOK OF MORMON

1 Nephi		5:18–19	145
3:20	145	10:17–19	99
5:11–14	146	13:23	147
5:13	145	17:45	168

Scripture Index

19:10	148	13:24–26	62
		19:4	8
2 Nephi		29:8	4
2:4	128	32:23	52, 182
3:11	79	32:28	168
4:2	148	32:34	123
26:28, 33	164	36:4	173
26:29	77	37:3	146
27:7–8, 10–11	143	37:4–5	146
28:29–30	114	39:19	52
28:30	122	43:2	110
28:31	119, 163		
29:8	141	Helaman	
29:13–14	147	8:19–20	148
31:5	179	8:20	153
31:15	174	9:16	8
32:5	91	11:18	8
Jacob		3 Nephi	
4:6	115	11:7	39
		11:32	80
Enos		12:6	134, 185
1:10	25	25:5–6	139
		26:3	144
Mosiah		26:6–7	144
3:3	164	26:6–11	143
3:4	133	29:5–6	119
4:3	165		
4:11	164	Mormon	
5:2	166	9:7–21	9
8:16–17	8	9:9	81
18:9–10	180	9:31	78
Alma		Ether	
5:11	8	4:4–7	143
5:47	185	15:33	144
12:9	5		
12:9–10	134	Moroni	
13:3–6	23	7:16	157
13:12	166	7:36–37	99
13:22	164	10:5	v, 163

DOCTRINE AND COVENANTS

1:4	132	3:4	78, 160
1:17–18	132	3:6–8	24
1:17–19	162	5:10	23
1:18	23	6:12	135
1:19–20	100	6:23	165
1:30	159	7:6	66
1:37	168, 174	8:2	166, 167
1:38	169	8:10	135
3:1	83	9:8	167, 168

10:52, 62	79	68:3–4	182
11:12–14	v	68:4	10, 116
11:25	119	75:4–5	162
13:1–2	65	76:5–10	108
17:6	142	76:15	135
18:34–36	185	76:20–21	40
20:9	179	76:94–95	188
20:11	79	76:100	153
20:77	181	77:11	68
27:5–14	92	77:14–15	66
27:12	80	82:10	174
29:11	61	84:6	36
31:3	164	84:6–16	29
31:4	23	84:7–13	148
32:45–47	123	84:13	153
36:4–7	42	84:14	35
37:5	44	84:17	93
38:32, 38	44	84:19	100, 152, 173
39:15	44		
42:11	23, 35, 81, 83	84:19–22	137
		84:20–25	76
42:14	11, 84, 171	84:23	121
43:7	35	84:23–25	94
43:16	24, 44	84:27	36
46:7	169	84:33–34	6
46:9	135	84:45–48	157
46:10–11	181	84:54–57	17
49:1	23	84:61	17
49:1, 4	162	84:63	44
49:4	23	84:63–64	181
49:14	99	86:10	141
50:2–4	85	88:6–12	166
50:9	85, 155	88:40	167
50:13–17	111	88:64–65	135
50:13–20	173	88:122	98
50:17–18	111	89:19	173
50:18, 20	91	93:2	157
50:19–20	113	93:6–18	149
50:23	133	93:12–14	122
50:24	123, 166	93:24–25	9, 175
52:9	184	93:27–28	175
52:14–19	86	93:28	91
56:4	123	93:36–37	177
60:2	181	93:39	177
60:2–3	24	93:49	43, 166, 187
63:7–11	161		
63:20–21	149	95:8–9	24, 44, 45
63:21–22	37	100:9–11	73
63:64	135	101:23–25	186
66:11	162	107:4	93
67:8	181	107:18–19	93, 137
67:9	166	107:19	100
67:10–13	76	107:30–31	173
67:11	113	107:48	32, 35
67:12	173	107:52	35

Scripture Index 215

107:53–56	92	124:40–42	42		
107:56	148	127:2	23		
107:56–57	153	128:19	173		
109:5	136	128:20–22	80		
109:12–13	136	130:3	96, 118		
109:12–13, 22, 26	44	130:18–19	174		
109:21–22	24	131:5–6	118, 177		
110:11	29	132:7	82		
110:11–16	80	132:19	118		
113:7–10	141	133:3	61		
121:26	173	133:24	151		
121:33	91	133:36–38	62		
121:36	76, 134	137:1–4	41		
121:42	173	138:1–2, 11	135		
121:45	173	138:53	44		
122:1–2	43				

PEARL OF GREAT PRICE

Moses
1:2, 11	31
1:4	141
1:11, 13–14	113
1:16–17	36
1:17, 25	31
1:39	132
4:2	162
5:9–12, 14	92
5:11	182
5:58	60
6:5	142
6:6–7	92
6:8	148
6:23	92
6:26–27	35
6:27	32
6:31	32, 73, 76
6:32–34	36
6:35	112
6:42	32, 35
7:27	60
7:3–4	32
8:19	35

Abraham
1:15–17	74
1:18–19	36
2:9, 11	43
3:11–12	33
3:15	33
3:22–23	26, 31, 33
3:27	162

Joseph Smith—Matthew
| 1:7 | 39 |
| 24:23 | 69 |

Joseph Smith—History
1:12	167
1:17	39
1:32	165
1:33	43
1:34	179
1:36–39	139
1:70	99
1:73	136
1:74	137

Articles of Faith
| 1:5 | 34, 42, 97 |
| 1:10 | 151 |